Using Qualitativ
Answer Your Res

Using Qualitative Methods to Answer Your Research Question

Open UP Study Skills

Paul Oliver

 Open University Press

Open University Press
McGraw Hill
8th Floor, 338 Euston Road
London
England
NW1 3BH

email: enquiries@openup.co.uk
world wide web: www.openup.co.uk

First edition published 2021

A catalogue record of this book is available from the British Library

ISBN-13: 9780335248957
ISBN-10: 0335248950
eISBN: 9780335248964

Library of Congress Cataloging-in-Publication Data
CIP data applied for

Typeset by Transforma Pvt. Ltd., Chennai, India

Praise Page

Oliver's book is an interesting and engaging personal introduction to qualitative research. It raises some important questions and would be a useful text for first time researchers on undergraduate courses or as a pre-course suggested reading for those starting postgraduate research programmes. Students are clearly introduced to different aspects of research and key ideas in relation to qualitative research methodology. The examples are interesting and easy to understand. The advice and case studies are applicable to researchers starting out. Therefore, the text is accessible and personal, including the reader as if part of the book's conversation.

Alaster Scott Douglas, Reader in Education and
Professional Practice, University of Roehampton, London, UK

Paul Oliver provides researchers with extensive, relevant and useful information around the scope, use and virtues of qualitative research. Accessible, clear and with the needs of the researcher in mind, this book ensures the fundamentals of qualitative research are explored through enthusiasm for the subject matter, an appreciation of the conceptual and philosophical underpinnings, as well as the practicalities of planning and conducting research.

Dr. Yunis Alam, Senior Lecturer in Sociology,
University of Bradford

Contents

Part I

The main features of qualitative methods

Part I

The main features of qualitative
methods

Chapter 1

Distinguishing between qualitative and quantitative methods

Chapter summary
In this chapter the differences between conducting research in the physical, material world and in the world of human beings and human interaction will be explored. Many of the terms mentioned in this chapter derive from philosophy and are outside the scope of everyday language. Ontology, which can be used to establish whether something exists, is examined, as well as bipolar terms, such as subjective and objective, qualitative and quantitative, positivism and anti-positivism. The relevance of existentialism and empiricism to research will also be discussed.

The difference between the physical world and the social world

When we return from a holiday, it is normal for our friends and family to ask us what it was like. They may ask us, for example, 'What was the weather like?' If we replied it was 'quite hot', or 'not very cold', they would probably press us by asking 'Well, what temperature was it?' They would expect us to give as precise an answer as we could, such as 25°C. They might also ask us about the nature of the resort, e.g. 'Was the hotel very friendly?' In reply, we might say, 'Oh yes, we got talking to lots of people, especially at dinner time.' However, we would probably be rather surprised if they followed on by asking us 'Well, how many people did you meet on Wednesday afternoon?'

These imaginary exchanges illustrate something of the difference between the *physical world* and the *social world*. Temperature is a feature of the physical world, and as such is susceptible to precise measurement. 'Friendliness', on the other hand, is more of a feature of the social world, and is normally much more difficult to measure precisely. We normally try to measure the physical world using numerical or quantitative measures, whereas we evaluate the social world using more descriptive or qualitative assessments.

When we consider the physical world, we tend to think of the kind of questions which are subsumed within disciplines such as chemistry, physics, astronomy or geology. Researchers in these subjects would tend to evaluate issues involving molecular structure, magnetic fields, or gravitational forces. Research would typically involve the taking of measurements of such phenomena as electrical resistance or friction between moving bodies. The data within such research would normally be quantitative, and the results would be expressed typically in the form of equations or statistical analysis. The aim of such research is usually to explain the occurrence of phenomena, and to predict the way in which the physical world might respond in the future. In quantitative investigations, researchers try to be as precise as possible in collecting data, and also in analysing that data.

However, not all research involves investigating the inanimate or physical world. We live in a very complex human society, and it is important that as far as possible we can understand the way in which human beings interact with each other. We are interested in questions such as how we can best educate the younger generation; why people commit crimes and how we can best respond to this; and how we can provide health care for an increasing population. When we start to think about research involving human beings, we realize that the situation is often very complex. We cannot simply use a measuring instrument to take some readings, and present these on a graph. We need to find other ways of collecting data. Often these methods involve talking to people, and reflecting carefully upon the things they say. So, for example, we might talk to elderly people about their health needs, and the ways in which people think these needs could be resolved. We might talk to previous offenders about the kind of social and other pressures which caused them to commit offences, and we might analyse the functioning of the justice system. The data from such research may not often be quantitative. It may much more typically involve words, and the collection of verbal accounts. Equally the analysis of such data may not lead to seemingly precise or concise results. The results may seem to be more general, and may suggest the collection and analysis of further data. Such qualitative research will usually require different data collection and analysis procedures when compared with quantitative methods.

Although the distinction between the physical world and the social world is very attractive, partly at least because of its apparent simplicity, it should at the same time be treated cautiously. A clear separation of the two is not as straightforward as it might seem. Human beings are part of the physical world in the sense that our bodies operate through a complex range of biochemical and molecular processes. Equally, human beings have a major impact upon the physical world through, for example, our environmental policies. There is, therefore, an argument to be made that the distinction between the physical world and the social world is more subtle and nuanced than might be assumed.

It follows then that in terms of research, it may be less helpful to think of a clear distinction between quantitative and qualitative methods, and to consider the use of a multi-methods approach. This would take into account the interaction between the physical and social worlds, and develop the use of research methods which combined qualitative and quantitative methods. This brief introduction, I hope, illustrates the fact that there is a wide range of issues here, and much room for debate. These issues affect both our view of the world around us, and the ways in which we conduct research into it. We now need to consider some of these questions in a little greater depth.

Advice for students 1.1

When you are writing your thesis, it is important that you do not select an approach to research, and then seek to justify this at all costs. It is generally considered better to discuss the complexity of the issues facing you, and then to explain in a balanced way the reasons for your choice of approach. This gives you an opportunity to demonstrate your understanding of research issues.

Ontology and our assumptions about reality

When we say that we are going to carry out a research investigation into a topic, there is a perhaps obvious assumption that the subject of the research actually exists: that we can collect data about it; and then analyse that data. It may seem strange to ask questions about whether or not something exists, but there is a branch of philosophy which does exactly that. This area of study is known as *ontology*, and it has important implications for research. Let us consider some examples.

Suppose that you want to research some aspects of bureaucracy. You are fairly clear what you mean by bureaucracy. You have in mind approaching a large organization for help or information, and it seems that lots of obstacles are put in your way. You think of this as bureaucracy. However, the ontological question is whether bureaucracy really exists out there in the world, and that it can be studied and measured; or whether it is simply a rather vague term which is difficult to define precisely. If bureaucracy as a concept actually exists, and can be measured accurately, then we speak of it as being realist in terms of its ontology. On the other hand, if we think of bureaucracy as being simply a name for a rather general idea, then we speak of it as having a nominalist ontology. Katz (2002: 261) pointed out that questions of ontology can be very useful in suggesting a direction for research to proceed.

To take another example, let us think of morality and ethics. For some people, moral principles such as justice, fair play and truth-telling are concepts which exist independently in the world. They are not, as such, issues which can be discussed and evaluated by individual people, but fixed notions which have been true for all time, and will continue to be so. If the latter is the case, then we would think of ethics as having a realist ontology. On the other hand, some people think of moral principles as being much more flexible. They think of them as being dependent upon individual circumstances or upon the context of a particular issue. In this case, what is deemed fair or otherwise is more a question of opinion, and will depend upon a whole range of factors which require careful consideration. If this is how we think of ethical issues, then it would be more relevant to speak of a nominalist ontology.

Subjectivism and objectivism

There are two other terms which are often used in the philosophy of research, and which are closely connected with *realism* and *nominalism*. These concepts are *objectivism* and *subjectivism*. A realist ontology tends to imply that when conducting research, you can identify precise concepts, ideas or factors and collect exact data upon them in an objective manner. Such data will be precisely measurable and could, for example, be collated on a spreadsheet or analysed mathematically. The assumption of objectivist research is that there would be broad agreement between researchers about the nature of the data which needed to be collected, and about how that data should be obtained. Personal opinion or judgement about the approach to the research would not be considered especially important. Objective research would assume a form of consensus about the nature of the research data and how it should be collected.

Suppose, for example, we are interested in investigating literacy levels, and in particular the understanding of vocabulary, among school children. It is decided to give the children a test constructed around the understanding of a passage of literature. There is the assumption that the test will measure what it is supposed to measure, and that it will be in a format so as to treat all children equally. This kind of approach assumes that research can be conducted in an objective and balanced manner.

A nominalist ontology, on the other hand, is much more subjective in its approach. It starts from the viewpoint that if you want to investigate literacy levels, there are a number of different ways of achieving this. Each research method will shed light on a different aspect of the issue, and researchers may well have their own preferences about how to approach the research. Different methods may have their own underlying philosophical assumptions, and researchers will make up their own minds concerning how to justify their own approach. The data from such a subjective approach may well typically be more qualitative than with an objective approach. It may be based upon records of interviews or discussions, for example, and different researchers may decide to analyse such data in a variety of ways.

Case study 1.1

It should be fairly clear from the discussion above, that the two broad approaches to ontology have implications for the type of research methodology you might select for your research study. If you start from realist assumptions about your research study, then you will be likely to employ measuring instruments or questionnaires, from which the data can be converted into numerical values. On the other hand, if your research is underpinned by nominalist assumptions, then you will be likely to collect data in the form of words. This could consist of interview transcripts, observational notes or autobiographical material. Thus, assumptions about ontology lead on logically to the selection of research methodology.

The existential debate: existence and essence

The debate about subjectivism and objectivism is further illustrated by a relatively contemporary school of thought known as *existentialism*. Its central ideas were raised initially by the Danish philosopher, Søren Kierkegaard (1813–1855), but it later became more generally associated with the French writer and philosopher, Jean-Paul Sartre (1905–80). As its name suggests, existentialism is concerned with the problems raised by the nature of human existence, and how we choose to conduct our lives.

One way of looking at this issue is to think of ourselves as being born with a certain genetic background, and in a particular social setting. These factors are seen as important in affecting both the type of person we become, and the role which we eventually have in life. Our lives then are seen as being significantly influenced by factors which are to a great extent outside our control. This view of the world is often known as *determinism*.

In the period during and just after the Second World War, Sartre challenged this view, and argued that human beings have much more freedom than is reflected in a deterministic view of the world. He argued that human beings are confronted with a wide range of choices in life, and have an obligation to make decisions, often involving moral choices, about the conduct of their lives. It is a disconcerting feature of the world that we are born into a situation where there is so much freedom. However, according to Sartre, we should think carefully about the ethical choices we make, and not to do so is to waste the freedom which we are given. Ultimately we have to take responsibility for our decisions, and for the nature of the lives which we lead. Existentialists view the world as not possessing any specific sense of meaning. The fundamental responsibility of human beings is to work out a sense of meaning for themselves and for the world at large. In this way they can take decisions about how to interact with other human beings and how to work towards creating a better world.

Existentialism is therefore more closely related to a subjectivist world-view. Much qualitative research is concerned with investigating the ways in which individual human beings attach meaning both to their world and to the world at large. In order to investigate meaning, researchers often need to conduct in-depth interviews, or to encourage respondents to write detailed personal accounts.

Sartre often summed up his philosophy by means of the short expression 'existence precedes essence'. By this, he meant that only after we are born do we begin to slowly create the essence of what we will become as a human being. After we acquire our existence, we begin to make the choices in our life which will give us our distinctive nature or essence. This idea had a profound effect upon post-war society in that it gave people an idea of the freedom which they possessed: the freedom to forge their own lives and existence. At the same time, in terms of social science research, it opened up the possibility of investigating the ways in which people made sense of their world. There is further discussion of this expression in Sartre (2007: 22).

Advice for students 1.2

Having read this chapter so far, you may be wondering whether it is really necessary to use these complex and esoteric terms such as ontology in your thesis. After all, if you are using interview research, for example, you may ask yourself whether these philosophical concepts have a place in your research account. Well, it certainly is not necessary to go into great detail about them, but a brief mention does allow you to demonstrate to your examiners that you have a grasp of the philosophical basis of your research. This is no bad thing, and it should help you to make a good impression with your work.

Epistemology and the kind of knowledge we hope to reveal

When we get to the end of a research study, I think that most researchers would like to believe that they know more about a subject than when they first started. Having collected a lot of data on a topic and devoted much time to its analysis, then they probably feel that they have added to the sum total of knowledge on a research question. However, the term 'knowledge' is what we call in research 'a problematic concept'. When we say that we 'know' something to be true, there are usually all kinds of factors which create a sense of uncertainty in our mind. To take an everyday example, we may say that we know that a bus leaves for town at 3.45 p.m. However, the reality is that the bus may leave slightly earlier, or later; it may not leave at all because there is a mechanical breakdown, a road traffic accident or a strike; or the time may have changed because of alterations in the bus timetable. These factors which may influence the reality of a situation are termed variables.

To take another example, suppose that a nurse studying for a higher degree wants to carry out research on the nurse role, in the hospital in which s(he) works. The researcher envisages using interview methods. However, as the research proceeds. it becomes evident that the existing work relationships between the researcher and other medical staff, are having an effect upon the data being collected. The interactions between the different clinical staff are so complex and varied, that the researcher finds it difficult to be precise about the nature of the knowledge being generated. The variety of social variables makes it difficult to draw precise conclusions. This is not to say that the task is impossible, but simply to appreciate that knowledge is not as clear-cut as might be expected.

Epistemology, therefore, is the study of the basis upon which we claim to know something, or believe something to be true. Darlaston-Jones (2007: 19) has stressed, for example, the significance of epistemology and its relevance for research methods. Since the process of acquiring knowledge is so complex, and the nature of knowledge so problematic, researchers need to be very careful about the implied degree of certainty they show in relation to knowledge. It is important to use words which do not imply a greater degree of certainty than is justified. For example, there are some words whose use can easily give the impression of unjustified certainty. In this context are words such as 'facts', 'proof', 'truth' and 'belief'. It is not too difficult to think of alternative words or expressions which avoid this implication of certainty. When you are writing your thesis, it would generally be better to avoid any implied certainty, so let us consider some alternatives.

When we use the term 'facts', we are suggesting that the information is uncontested. That is, that a range of researchers would all treat the information as having the same degree of validity. It would be better to use words or expressions which are neutral in terms of validity, or leave room for a degree of interpretation. The word 'data' is frequently used by researchers to refer, for example, to the outcome of interviews. You could also say that 'the results of the interviews suggest that …' since this leaves some room for interpretation.

For similar reasons, the words 'proof', 'proved' and 'truth' are best avoided in accounts of research. They suggest that the researcher has reached an absolute, definite conclusion after analysing research data, and yet we just cannot be so certain. There is usually room for interpretation and discussion concerning the certainty of knowledge. For preference, you could use an expression such as 'the results of the data analysis give the impression that …' This again allows for interpretation, or for amending one's conclusions in the light of further evidence.

The word 'belief' is also normally unsuitable for use in accounts of research. It can give the impression that we have excluded the possibility of further evidence or data. It is important with any research conclusion that we leave open the possibility of amending the results if we find data to the contrary. In summary, then, researchers have always to bear in mind the provisional nature of their findings, and the possibility that these findings will need to be amended in the face of further data.

Positivism and anti-positivism

Epistemological approaches to research are usually divided into *positivism* and *anti-positivism* (see Meyers, 2014: 4, for further discussion of epistemology). Positivism, which is derived from a realist ontology, assumes that there are realities in the world which can be accurately measured. This approach to epistemology was first articulated by the French philosopher, Auguste Comte (1798–1857), and later extended and amplified by a French sociologist, Émile Durkheim (1858–1917). Positivists take the view that just as entities such as mass, acidity, pressure or electric current exist in the physical world, and can be measured using units of measurement, then entities exist in the social world too, and these can also be measured as part of a research process. The entities in the social world might be such factors as aristocracy, social integration, power, or religious belief. Part of the assumption of the positivist viewpoint is that sociologists can stand back from the social world and take measurements or collect data in an objective manner.

Anti-positivism, however, is associated with a nominalist ontology, and takes a very different view of the social world. For the anti-positivist, there are no specific social entities which can be measured. In this perspective the researcher cannot stand back dispassionately from society, and measure aspects of it. Human beings are seen as the creators of society, by virtue of their continual interaction with it. Society does not exist externally to human beings, but rather society and humanity are an integrated whole. In order to study society, the researcher needs to investigate human interaction and the nature of social meaning and understanding which emerges from that. Within this frame of reference, researchers do not measure society as such, but try to understand its complexities and subtleties. Clarke (2009: 29) has pointed out that the social world is permeated by reflective individuals, whereas data from the physical sciences is not, by its nature, reflective.

Generally speaking, positivist researchers collect data which is quantitative in character. This may involve the use of measuring instruments or questionnaires, and analytic procedures which convert the data into a statistical form. Anti-positivist researchers normally collect data which is in verbal form and use analytic procedures which try to reveal meaning and significance in the data. As such qualitative research involves a good deal of interpretation of data, anti-positivism is often known as *interpretivism*, or as an interpretivist approach.

Empiricism as a method of investigation

Finally, in this discussion of the nature of knowledge, and of the extent to which we can be certain that we know something to be true, we need to consider the term 'empiricism'. The concept of *empiricism* is frequently found in research accounts, typically where the researcher uses phrases such as 'there is empirical evidence that …', or 'the empirical data collected so far suggests that …'.

During the seventeenth and eighteenth centuries there was an increasing argument that the only valid knowledge was derived from the evidence collected by our senses. Hossain (2014: 225) reiterated this, pointing out that empiricism rejected notions of instinctive understanding. In other words, if we could see, feel or touch something in the world, then we could use that evidence or data as the basis for drawing valid conclusions. For example, if two pieces of metal were rubbing together, and we could detect a rise in temperature, then we could begin to understand something of the nature of friction. People who took this position were known as empiricists, and a well-known early advocate was John Locke (1632–1704). An alternative view about knowledge is *idealism*. People who hold this view argue that the only valid knowledge is that emerging from mental reasoning. Suppose we consider the question 'Is cruelty towards people always bad?' An empiricist would probably investigate this issue by observing many instances of cruelty and then trying to analyse whether the consequences were always adverse. An idealist, on the other hand, would probably argue that this process is unnecessary. Cruelty by its very nature is immoral and unkind, and we know this from the very nature of the concept. We do not need to collect lots of empirical data to establish this. It is self-evident from the idea of cruelty.

The empirical method in relation to knowledge was increasingly associated with the development of science and with the Industrial Revolution. There was an appreciation of the power of scientific thinking and of the contribution which this could make to society. Although empiricism is often closely linked with positivism and the scientific method, it is important to realize that its relevance is wider than that. Empiricism is equally as applicable to qualitative research. If we observe people interacting in a social situation, the data we collect as observational notes is empirical in just the same way as if we collected quantitative data. Making observations depends upon the use of our senses, and hence is empirical in nature. Philosophers and researchers often use the term *a posteriori* to describe a situation where we collect data first, and then draw conclusions about the world. The opposite of this is *a priori* reasoning where we use our powers of reasoning to draw conclusions before we have collected any empirical or sense evidence.

In principle, then, if we collect quantitative or qualitative data, and use this as the basis of trying to understand the world, we are thinking empirically, and using *a posteriori* reasoning. This is the basis of what we normally refer to as scientific thought. However, *a priori* reasoning still has a very important function in research. When we are planning a research project of any kind, we normally need to consider the concepts which we will use to design the research aims and analysis. Suppose, for example, that we are planning a research study designed to investigate whether an examination system has become more difficult in recent years. One of the key issues to be resolved here, before we even think of the type of data to collect, is the question of how we will define the concept 'difficult'. For example, we may decide to investigate whether a broader range of knowledge is required because of changes in the curriculum; we may wish to investigate whether students are now required to carry out more interpretation of information rather than simple recall; or we may wish to investigate the systems of assessment, such as the balance between essay writing and textual analysis. In other words, the 'difficulty' of an examination is a complex issue, and in order to carry out research in this area, we will almost certainly need to define what we mean by the term before we start to collect data.

This process of definition or conceptual analysis is at least partially an *a priori* process. While our analysis of the concept of difficulty may rely in part upon our previous experience of the examination process, the process of conceptual clarification depends also upon cognitive analysis. Some examinations, for example, may depend upon the writing of essays as a means of assessment. However, we would need to analyse exactly what this is testing. Essays may test the ability to recall information, to structure and analyse information, to compare and contrast information, to write in an elegant prose style, or indeed many other qualities. Therefore, before we begin to collect data on the balance of essay writing in an examination, or on its effectiveness in terms of assessment, we need to analyse the overall purpose of including essay questions.

In research, as in many other aspects of life, we do tend to think in terms of binary divisions such as qualitative and quantitative, subjective and objective, or *a priori* and *a posteriori*. This type of thinking can be very useful, in the sense that it helps us to be clear about the type of process which we are employing in research. However, it can be argued that this binary thought system is an over-simplification of the research process, and that research often benefits from using a combination of positivist and interpretive thinking.

Case study 1.2

Suppose that we are embarking on a research project entitled 'The consequences of punishment in prison on rates of recidivism'. From what we have argued earlier, we would probably need to analyse the concepts of 'punishment' and of 'recidivism' before proceeding with data collection. However, as the research title employs the term 'rates of recidivism' it seems reasonable that we would collect quantitative data on this, and then analyse it statistically. It is possible that there might be a need for some qualitative data, but the emphasis will probably be upon quantitative analysis.

However, if the research title is altered to 'the attitudes of prisoners to changes in the punishment regime', then we may well feel that the emphasis has changed from the measurement of external 'facts' to the analysis of feelings in relation to external factors such as punishment systems. Overall, this revised title seems to lend itself to the collection of qualitative data, through the use of observations or interviews with prisoners.

This is not to say that, in either case, a combination of methods would not be possible, but the emphasis of one or the other would depend on the nature of the research question.

The terms and concepts used in this chapter are largely derived from philosophy, and provide a framework for thinking about the research process. In your thesis, when you are discussing the planning of your research, it will be very useful to employ some of these concepts, as it will demonstrate that you have thought clearly about the underlying basis of your project. We will now move on in Chapter 2 to discuss some of the main features of qualitative and interpretive research.

Learning content

In this chapter you should have become familiar with the following ideas:

- *a priori* and *a posteriori* knowledge
- epistemology, positivism and anti-positivism
- existentialism and research
- realism and nominalism in ontology
- subjectivism and objectivism
- the nature of empiricism
- the nature of the physical world and the social world

Chapter **2**

Interpretive research and the scientific paradigm

Chapter summary
In this chapter you will explore the role of interpretive research in trying to make sense of human experience, and to understand the ways in which people generate a feeling of meaning in relation to society. You will engage with ideas such as the social construction of knowledge, phenomenology, and the differences between holism and reductionism in research. The chapter ends with a taxonomy of research methods to help guide you through the sometimes complex terminology of research.

The nature of interpretation in research

The idea of accurate measurement was central to the positivist view of the world. It was felt in the mid-nineteenth century that anything was susceptible to precise measurement as long as the research was planned in the correct way. The assumptions of the positivist approach were that researchers understood the variables which required measurement, and that they were able to stand back from the measurement process and conduct their research in a balanced and objective manner. The idea of 'distance' between researchers and the object of their research was important to positivists because it served to underline the possibility of impartiality and independence in research.

When designing a bridge, for example, architects could calculate the likely stresses on the main spans of the structure, the likely forces generated by adverse weather conditions, and the most appropriate construction materials for a particular design. The possibility of working in this objective rationalist manner gave the impression to researchers during the Victorian period that it was in principle possible to control the natural world and to have access to almost unlimited technological development. There was, however, the gradual realization that the subject-object division between researchers and the problem being researched was not only impossible, but also undesirable.

Let us consider examples from two different areas: education and health. Suppose we are researching the efficacy of a new method of computer-mediated learning in higher education, with a view to students working more independently. From a positivist point of view, we may decide to compare a group of students working in the traditional manner supported by a tutor, with a group working independently using computer-based learning methods. We may try to eliminate extraneous variables such as the academic background of students by selecting groups which had similar qualifications and professional experience. However, it may be very difficult to control the large number of potential variables.

Interpretive researchers, on the other hand, may start from a very different perspective. Rather than trying to measure the impact of a new educational initiative, they may decide to investigate the feelings of students working more independently with less support from a tutor. They may ask the students to describe whether they found it difficult to access information, whether it was difficult to resolve problems on their own without the advice of a tutor, or whether they experienced feelings of isolation. By talking to students and trying to tease out their underlying emotions, interpretive researchers would try to understand and document the deeper reactions of students, and to gradually construct a picture of what it was like to work in a different way.

The purpose of *interpretive research* is therefore less about attempts at objective measurement and more about trying to make sense of the human experience. It is also important to note that the positivist approach starts with decisions about what needs to be measured. Interpretive researchers argue that this approach is arbitrary in that the decisions reflect not objective research decisions, but the personal prejudices or ideological preferences of the researchers. The interpretive position is to start with much more of a blank slate in terms of formulating ideas, and to work towards an understanding of how the students are affected by a new method of studying. Further discussions of interpretive research designs may be found in Schwartz-Shea and Yanow (2012: 5).

Advice for students 2.1

When beginning a qualitative study, you clearly need some plan for beginning the data collection process. However, where you commence and with whom is not quite as critical as with positivist research. As the data collection process proceeds, you can adjust your sampling depending upon the nature of the data you are receiving, and also the availability of suitable respondents.

In an analogous situation in a hospital where a new system of nursing care was introduced, positivist researchers would try to investigate its usefulness by measuring such variables as length of stay of patients, clinical indicators of the body's function, and perhaps satisfaction gradings given by patients and their relatives. Again, it is the researcher, however, who decides on what is to be measured. The interpretive approach would be to encourage the patients to define what for them are the critical issues in the care process, and what needs to be evaluated.

Unlike the positivist approach with its separation of researcher and object of research, interpretive researchers see themselves as inextricably linked with the respondents who are providing data. Within interpretivism, the researcher and respondent are seen as being linked in a joint enterprise of trying to understand the social world, as discussed by Tadajewski (2006: 430). Wherever possible, preconceptions are avoided, and there is a sense of working together to add to our understanding of whether a new initiative is likely to be effective.

The interpretive approach tends to view a form of dialectic existing between the researcher and the respondents who are providing the data. In the case of investigating a new initiative, the respondents will have their own perceptions of the new process, and at the same time the researchers will have developed their own viewpoint. There will almost inevitably be a degree of interaction between the two sets of interpretation. Each will influence the other, and will help generate a range of new data which emerges from the dialectical process.

It is important also to note that positivists tend to view data collection as a process fixed in time. Although they may repeat the process some time later, they tend to view data collection as a single, separate process where the data, once collected, is analysed, and the research process regarded as completed, at least for the time being. The philosophy of the interpretive process is very different, however. It views research as continuing into the future, with a continual process of interaction between researcher and respondent. Each continues to influence the other in a gradual process of refinement of the data collection and analysis.

An important element of this iterative process is that the respondents can manage, in the data which they provide, to give as accurate a picture of their views as possible. If you have ever been asked to complete an evaluation form of some type, you will probably have been frustrated by the impossibility of choosing responses which accurately reflect your feelings and opinions. The questions and alternative responses have been pre-structured by the researchers and consequently reflect *their* opinions and values, and not yours. This highlights one of the great difficulties of positivist research. It almost inevitably imposes external values upon the respondents.

Another facet of this phenomenon is the use of numerical rating scales when gathering data. It is very tempting to try to gather data using numerical scales as it gives an impression of precision and accuracy. Statistical operations can be conducted on the data and this gives a sense of understanding of a phenomenon. However, interpretivists argue that such approaches are reductionist in the sense that they over-simplify complex phenomena. For example, if we ask respondents to grade their feelings about something in terms of being good to bad, useful to not useful, or helpful to unhelpful, using a scale of 1 to 5, there is an assumption that we actually know what a grade of 2, or a grade of 4 represents. We may know that 3 is better than 2, but it is difficult to be certain that we know what they actually represent. Interpretivists argue that the use of numbers in this way is a form of delusion and gives only an impression of accuracy. They feel that it is much more accurate to ask respondents to represent their feelings in words, even if this requires a much longer description. Suppose, for example, that we ask a group of people to read a novel. We would be very surprised if they all had the same opinion of the plot and the characters. We would expect there to be widely divergent opinions. This takes us on to the question of meaning, and the way in which human beings create a sense of understanding and significance about the social world.

Exploring meaning within social interaction

If we think for a moment about the way in which people understand the world, it is likely that research respondents will be influenced by a wide variety of factors. Their genetic inheritance, their upbringing, political views, economic status and occupational history, are just some of the factors which are likely to influence their view of the world, and their perception of the world around them. Interpretive researchers are very interested in the way this complex of factors provides a sense of meaning and understanding. In order to comprehend *social meaning*, interpretive researchers feel that the most appropriate way is to encourage respondents to describe their vision of the world. This is seen as the best way to gather data which is valid.

In social research, when we speak of the *validity* of data, this has a specific meaning. It refers to the extent to which data actually represents the reality of what it claims to represent. For example, suppose that we ask a school-teacher about the most difficult aspect of their job. The reality may be that the greatest difficulty is with keeping discipline among the students. However, they may not wish to admit that they find difficulty in this area, because they feel that they might be perceived as incompetent. Therefore, they may claim that the most difficult facet is keeping up to date with subject matter. This is perhaps something which is less contentious and which can be relatively easily remedied through a range of staff development programmes. The point about this is that the response does not reflect a high level of validity. The problem could be even greater if the question were asked by someone in a management position, or someone in an inspectorial role who was capable of having an adverse effect upon the career progression of the teacher.

Such problems are complex when quantitative data is being collected. Suppose that we ask the same question as above about the most difficult feature of the job and then offer a number of alternative responses as defined by the researcher. The respondent is asked to tick the response which is nearest to their opinion. The number of the response provides a range of quantitative data which can be analysed. However, as there is only a limited range of pre-defined responses, it will be difficult for the respondents to choose an alternative which is close to their feelings. In other words, the responses will have low validity.

Qualitative researchers, however, feel that they are able, through a process of detailed questioning, to get much closer to the truth about an issue and to elicit responses which have a high validity. In the above example, if the researcher does not feel that the first response about subject knowledge has high validity, then they can try gradually to explore other areas such as discipline to gauge the reaction of a respondent. In this sense, the researcher is able to generate responses of a higher validity, through a gradual process of question and answer. While it is true that the data from such a process may be very detailed, and not necessarily easy to summarize, nevertheless it should have a reasonably high level of validity and should represent the actual feelings of the respondents.

The concept of meaning is very important in understanding the way in which research respondents interact with each other to construct a social world. When a small group of people gather together on a social occasion, they may each express a range of views about, say, a political issue. Providing that each person is reasonably open-minded, then they will be influenced to some extent by the views expressed and may adapt their own views. As opinions continue to be exchanged, there may gradually emerge a new social reality which incorporates the different perspectives of the participants. The documentation of this process and the understanding of how it operates in reality is an important function of qualitative research. It is particularly relevant to qualitative methods, since to understand the interplay of exchanges of meaning, it is necessary to document the conversational processes in great detail. On such occasions, we are observing the construction of new worlds of social understanding, during which people's sense of meaning changes. Such interpretive research has been particularly associated with the views of the German sociologist, Max Weber (1864–1920).

Of course, one might argue that not all human interactions are open-minded and receptive to new and different views on society. Some people, for various reasons, embrace relatively fixed views on issues, and are reluctant, if not unable, to change them. In such cases we may refer to this as an example of ideology. Cochran-Smith and Fries (2001: 3–4) suggest ways in which *ideology* may be employed in evaluating educational issues. When someone possesses a fixed world-view and regards all issues and questions which they reflect on, within the scope of that world-view, then it is difficult to encourage them to think about something in an open, rational way. If someone appears to be operating from an ideological viewpoint, then it may be very difficult to convince them of this. The very fact that they have, or appear to have, a closed world-view, makes it by definition very difficult to open up their thought processes to rational analysis.

We tend to find ideological thought particularly in such spheres as politics and religion, where a single world-view or belief system may be so all-embracing, that for such an individual all questions are considered within the principles, beliefs, thoughts, knowledge and ways of reasoning associated with that ideology. We may bemoan the fact that it is difficult to change the views of such a person or to encourage them to think within the parameters of scientific rationalism.

Advice for students 2.2

There is no reason in principle why a researcher should not conduct research and write a research thesis from the perspective of a particular ideology. For example, you may choose to conduct your research project using a Marxist perspective. This would in principle be acceptable, but with one important caveat. This is that you include in the thesis a reflective account which discusses your particular perspective, and explains the impact this has had on the conduct of the research. This renders your approach open and transparent.

However, a further complication relevant to research is whether rationalism is itself an ideology. It can be argued that whenever we look at the world, whatever our particular viewpoint, we reflect our own specific world-view. This, it can be argued, has developed through a wide variety of factors, and reflects a unique manner of thinking. Within this viewpoint, we all think in an ideological manner, and there is therefore an unavoidable bias in our interpretation of the world. If we assume then that all research is to an extent biased and reflects individual viewpoints, we may consider that the entire research process is flawed. However, one solution to this dilemma is to reflect upon our own possible biases, and to try in an open and transparent manner to illuminate our own way of thinking. In this way we may not eliminate all bias and ideological thought, but at least we expose the limitations of our reasoning process.

The social construction of understanding and knowledge

The pursuit of absolute truth is an attractive proposition. It can give us the feeling that there exist in the world fixed ideas, whether moral, political, aesthetic or religious, which are certain and valid for all times and all places. If we accept the possibility of such ideas, then the world seems a much more certain place, and perhaps filled with a greater sense of security. However, the proposition that there exist ideas which are eternally true, carries as its corollary and consequence the proposition that there also exist ideas which are fundamentally flawed. Not all ideas can be absolutely true and valid, since some ideas exist clearly in opposition to one another. We are therefore forced into asking ourselves the very difficult question, 'On what grounds can we assert that one idea is superior to another idea?' Further discussion of the concept of *social construction* is available in Gergen (2015: 4).

One possible solution to this dilemma is to apply a form of *consequentialism* to the problem. In the case of economic theory, for example, suppose we are trying to determine whether a socialist economic system or a free-market system is the most effective. We may apply both systems in a reasonably comparable context, and then observe the consequences for the population at large. We would try to judge which economic system generally had the best effects for society as a whole. However, in reality, this may be a very difficult issue to resolve. In other words, trying to create a hierarchy of ideas, from the best to the worst, may actually raise more complex problems than it resolves.

The other solution to this problem is to resign oneself to the notion that trying to construct a sequence of ideas from the most to the least valid, will be likely to fail. One possible solution, and the one which is generally favoured by qualitative researchers, is to accept a form of epistemological relativism. This is the argument that, generally speaking, all ideas are approximately equal in value and validity. I say approximately because some people may find it very difficult to accept the equality of some ideas. Suppose, for example, that two judges are faced by someone convicted of petty theft. One wishes to impose a long prison sentence, while the other suggests a period of community service. Most people may feel that in contemporary society, the latter course of action is the wisest.

Nevertheless, the general principle of epistemological relativism is that ideas exist in relation to a particular social system or world-view. The concept of relativism derives from the way in which we suppose that knowledge is created. In the case of *a priori* knowledge, this may be generated by cognitive reflection on a problem, without, in principle, the need for empirical evidence. On the other hand, *a posteriori* knowledge is generated largely from the analysis of empirical data. The concept of relativism is derived from an alternative view of the way in which knowledge is generated. Kinzel and Kusch (2018: 41), for example, point out the different perceptions of philosophers and sociologists towards relativism.

The sociology of knowledge approach rests upon the assumption that all forms of knowledge are influenced in their development by the social context in which they evolve. If we live, for example, in a society which is governed by warrior-kings, and which is subject to military conventions, it would not be difficult to understand if legal infringements within that society are subject to severe physical punishment, or even capital punishment. However, in a more liberal society governed by a form of civil democracy and the rule of law, one might expect to see more reformative types of justice. Now as there are no criteria against which we can judge these two forms of justice, all we can do is to consider them within the perspective of the society in which they have developed. Neither is right, and neither is wrong. They merely represent different forms of justice, which are related to their social context. This perspective on the world is sometimes termed *cultural relativism*. That is, cultures, knowledge, ideas, economic systems and political systems are not absolutely right or wrong, but can only be seen in comparison to each other and to the social contexts in which they exist.

However, if we say that all world-views are equal, this leaves us with a complex philosophical problem, and that is 'How can we decide between different courses of action?' Since we regard all aspects of knowledge as broadly equal, it is very difficult to resolve questions, whether ethical, psychological or philosophical. All we can do is to make an intuitive judgement and perhaps to justify it on the *a priori* grounds. We see here the rather uncomfortable relationship between *a priorism* and *a posteriorism*. To some extent, they are both interconnected.

Although the creation or construction of knowledge can be seen as related to the particular social setting, the actual mechanism by which this takes place exists on an interpersonal level. If a group of people are discussing a political debate on television, there will probably be a wide range of opinions expressed. At the end of the discussion some people may find that they have revised their opinion of the political question, while others may feel that their opinion has been consolidated. The group of people here have gone through a process of social construction, in which extra layers of knowledge have been accumulated between them, along with the construction of a wider level of understanding. One can view this as a process during which individuals build up their own vision of the world, and at the same time are influenced by the social world around them. During this process of social construction, multiple visions of the world are in competition with each. Ultimately some will succeed in becoming widespread and popular, and other perspectives will be less popular.

It is also worth noting, however, that within a relativistic perspective, world-views do not remain fixed and rigid. Competing world-views are part of a dynamic social process which, in a sense, is never completed. There is an ever-changing social process which first favours one perspective, and then favours another. The result is a dynamic society which in principle should be able to adapt to a range of circumstances.

Case study 2.1

In a research study involving interactions between different people, some form of interview methodology may be appropriate. This would enable the development of different viewpoints to be explored, with a view to analysing the ways in which each person's developing world-view affects those in the remainder of the group.

A holistic approach to research

The idea of a multi-faceted view of society or the world is linked to the concept of *holism* in research. Holism views society as consisting of a wide range of different processes which are in a constant state of interaction, working together in order to produce a coherent whole. According to holists, in order to understand society, it would be counter-productive to attempt to study individual processes and to understand how each process affects society as a whole. What is really important is to understand the system of collaborative working whereby systems inter-relate to produce an integrated society. Within holism, the totality of society is seen as more significant than the combination of the different functioning elements of which society is composed. Morse and Chung (2003 : 18) argue that it can be advantageous to employ several different qualitative methods in conjunction, in order to enhance the possibility of a holistic approach.

When you start to develop a research question for your thesis, it is quite normal for the question to begin as a fairly broad issue. You will probably be advised to narrow this down to a more precise question. Inevitably research has to be concerned with fairly precise issues, but there is an inherent danger here. Suppose that you decide to investigate aspects of the way in which young children learn to read. You may decide to focus upon the contribution of parents to the process of learning to read. This is fine as long as you do not lose sight entirely of the other factors, such as the work done in school, the teaching methods used, the types of books chosen for practice and the way in which reading practice is structured.

If we take a broad research question and focus on only one facet of this, then this is known as reductionism. The problem with reductionism is that the research becomes so specific that it is in danger of ignoring the many other aspects of, in this case, learning to read. There needs to be a continual effort to relate your narrowed research to the other aspects of the broad issue, and hence to take a holistic view.

The same is true of methodology. In the above example, you may decide as your principal research strategy to interview a sample of parents concerning the help they give their children each evening, in supplementing the reading practice done at school. This would give a qualitative focus to your research, and you could legitimately claim in the title of your thesis, that this was a qualitative study. However, it would be perfectly reasonable to include some quantitative measures in your thesis, providing evidence of the progress of the children in terms of reading. You could argue that such an approach was more holistic than relying exclusively upon interviews.

The phenomenological perspective

As we examine some of the underlying principles of qualitative research, then *phenomenology* is often regarded as one of the most important bases of the approach. Founded initially upon the philosophical writings of Edmund Husserl (1859–1938), it concentrates upon trying to illuminate the ways in which the individual person perceives the world around them. In particular, the phenomenological research process tries to set on one side the assumptions which we all hold about the social world. For example, if we are investigating the attitudes of mature students to university study, we may come across preconceptions which see higher education as something too complex for the 'ordinary' person. The phenomenological approach tries to explore in detail some of the factors which have led to this viewpoint. Such research often involves a slow and detailed examination of the background of the respondent, and the way in which this affects their view of the world.

In order to reveal this kind of data, phenomenology normally uses a very small number of respondents, even sometimes just a single person. Only in this way can time be devoted to obtaining the very detailed data which is needed to explore the deeper feelings and experiences of people. The most typical approach to the gathering of data involves established qualitative methods such as interviews and discussions. Also, when researchers are engaging with the respondent, they try not to be directive in the way that they explore a topic. They will normally introduce a topic for discussion and try to allow the respondent to select the direction in which the discussion goes. The emphasis is as far as possible upon revealing the world-view of the respondent.

Case study 2.2

Suppose that you wish to research the professional life history of a senior police officer. You are interested in the social and legal changes which have taken place during the officer's career, and would like to explore how they view these changes and their impact upon their professional existence. You could adopt an oral history or autobiographical approach to the collection of data, but embedded within the theoretical principles of phenomenology. The use of the latter concepts would provide a strong theoretical position, which would usefully strengthen the study, particularly if it were at doctoral level.

Just as the approach encourages respondents to set on one side their previous notions about a subject, there is also the question of the embedded assumptions of the researcher. The latter, just like the respondent, arrives at the research situation with a range of ideas, motivations, inclinations and other assorted psychological attitudes. It is important that the researcher is aware of this, and takes steps to minimize the consequences for the research. One strategy would be that through a process of self-reflection the researcher acknowledges and discusses during the research process, the psychological aspects of his or her personality which are relevant to the research. This then renders the research process more transparent. The alternative approach is for the researcher to try to identify key features of his or her thinking, and then to try to reduce the consequences by taking a variety of steps, such as perhaps avoiding a specific topic during the interviews, or by not being too intense in the questioning process in relation to a particular issue.

As a related issue, it is important for researchers to be aware of the impact and effect of cultural issues upon the lifestyle of both researchers and respondents. In an ideal world, phenomenological research tries to overlook features of culture and lifestyle. While it is not always possible to achieve this, such features can be incorporated in a reflective or reflexive account in a thesis, which seeks to discuss them and in a transparent way explore their possible effects upon the research.

Different perceptions of the social world

Advances in knowledge in quantitative research and in qualitative research take place in fundamentally different ways. In positivism, the researcher proposes a provisional statement about some feature of the world. This is known as a hypothesis. The researcher then develops a strategy for collecting data, in order to investigate whether that data seems either to support or negate the working hypothesis. If the data supports the hypothesis, then the latter is provisionally accepted; if not, then the hypothesis is amended in the light of the data, and further data is collected in order to re-test the hypothesis. This method of proceeding in research is known as deduction, or as the hypothetico-deductive principle.

The alternative approach, and the one associated with qualitative research, is known as induction. In this process the researcher collects data on a particular subject of interest. Often there is no pre-ordained plan to the data gathering. Rather, after the first section of data is collected and analysed, the researcher gains ideas for the next data collection procedure. This continues until the researcher feels that they have sufficient data with which to develop a provisional theory. This theory is then subjected to testing through the collection of new data. As a result of this, the theory may be provisionally accepted, or it may be developed and enriched by virtue of the new data. Within this model of induction, the researcher never really reaches the point at which the theory is totally accepted. There is always the possibility that new data may be found which will negate the theory, and for this reason the theory always remains provisional.

Within the deductive approach, there tends to be a more precise focus to the collection of data, since the purpose is to test a specific hypothesis. The method lends itself to the collection of quantitative data, or we could say numerical data, since such empirical measurements are suited to the evaluation of a precise hypothesis. In such cases, the data is often analysed statistically in order to try to determine the limits within which the data may be said to support or negate the hypothesis.

In qualitative research, however, as the inductive method does not demand, at least in the initial stages, a highly predetermined data collection schedule, then there tends to be a much wider range of data collection methods used. The following section provides an overview of this variety of methods. The taxonomy which follows is intended to illustrate some of the similarities and differences between quantitative and qualitative methods. It should provide you with a fairly succinct statement which shows the variety of strategies whereby qualitative methods may be used to address your research question.

A taxonomy of research methods

The terminology of social research methods is very complex, and I hope that at this stage of the book this taxonomy will provide you with a guide to which you can turn in order to remind yourself of some of the main terms and concepts. Although this book is devoted to the richness and depth provided by qualitative methods when addressing research questions, it should be helpful to keep in mind some of the contrasting positions of qualitative and quantitative methods (Table 2.1).

Table 2.1 Comparison of quantitative and qualitative research

Quantitative research	Qualitative research
Primarily conducted in the material, physical world	Primarily conducted in the human, social world
Aspires to achieve an objective stance	Aspires to achieve a subjective stance
Based on a positivist epistemology	Based on an anti-positivist, interpretive epistemology
Adopts an empirical approach	Adopts an empirical approach
Employs a hypothetico-deductive approach	Employs an inductive approach
Often uses statistical analysis to test hypotheses	Often uses inductive analysis to generate theory
Tends to employ larger-scale probability sampling	Tends to employ smaller-scale non-probability sampling
Tends towards absolutism in terms of ideas	Tends towards relativism in terms of ideas
Methodology tends to be restricted to mathematical measurement and questionnaires	Wide variety of methodologies used, such as: • Phenomenology • Interviews • Ethnography • Life history • Autobiography • Symbolic interactionism • Participant observation • Case study research • Action research • Feminism
Data is largely numerical	Data is largely verbal

Learning content

In this chapter you should have become familiar with the following ideas:

- consequentialism
- cultural relativism
- holism
- ideology
- interpretive research
- phenomenology
- social construction of knowledge
- social meaning
- validity

Part  II

The reasons for using qualitative methods

Part II

The reasons for using qualitative methods

Chapter 3

Research questions and the interpretive paradigm

> **Chapter summary**
> In this chapter you will appreciate the range of research questions which can be addressed through qualitative methods. A discussion of the nature of induction is followed by an exploration of the creation of new social theory. There is an analysis of the use of interpretivism in research on ethnicity, in understanding issues of power and inequality in research, and in feminist approaches to research. Finally, there is a discussion of postmodernism, and the implications of this for interpretive methodologies.

Varieties of research questions

If you meet someone who is studying for a research degree and ask them the subject of their research, they may only give you a brief answer. They may say, for example, that it is 'on immigration'. If you press them further on the subject, they may say, 'well, it is a study of the sociology of immigration'. This only gives you a general idea of the broad topic of the study, and does not tell you anything about the details of the research process. Only if you engaged the person in further conversation would you be likely to discover the real details of the study. When you are planning a research study, first, you need to be able to formulate it in terms of the precise purposes of the research, and, second, it is necessary to express these in the form of a title for your thesis.

When you are formulating a research question, there are a number of different issues to consider. Many of these issues raise very practical concerns to which the researcher needs to formulate a practical response. Suppose that in the above example, the purpose of the research is to gather data from Syrian immigrants on the physical and psychological trauma experienced during their travels in Europe in search of a safe domicile. A number of questions then pose themselves. How will the researcher make contact with such immigrants? How will the researcher identify the immigrants as of Syrian origin? Will there be language communication difficulties, and how will these be surmounted? What sample size does the researcher envisage being required?

In the case of the last issue, this topic may tend to lend itself to a qualitative study. Quantitative research often requires relatively large sample sizes because of the subsequent need to analyse data statistically. In the above example, however, where there might well be the need to employ interpreters and translators, there might be practical difficulties in collecting data from a large sample. It would be much more practical to work with a restricted sample and hence employ a qualitative approach. In addition, with a smaller sample of respondents, it would be easier to confirm their country of origin, and to gather data on the situation in their region of origin.

The nature of the proposed study suggests that the target population may be fairly dispersed, and hence there may be some difficulties in identifying respondents, and obtaining permission from them to take part in the research project. Moreover, there remains the issue of the methods employed to contact respondents. This might involve visits to refugee camps, or contacts arranged via charitable agencies in the country of final settlement. In addition, if the proposed purpose of the research is to gather data on the traumas associated with being a refugee, then the data collection process is likely to be most effective where the researcher is known and trusted by the respondents. The most appropriate methodology would appear to be one in which in-depth discussions took place between the respondents and the researcher. In other words, a qualitative approach would seem to be the most relevant.

A further aspect of any research project is the issue of whether members of the research sample will actually provide the amount or level of data required. One can imagine that refugees who have been through extremely traumatic circumstances may not necessarily wish to talk in detail about those experiences. Before investing a large amount of time in a research study, it is wise for the researcher to satisfy themselves that the respondents are willing to help with the study, and fully understand what will be expected of them during the research. It is very important from a moral point of view that respondents fully appreciate the nature of the research project, so that they may decide in advance if there are any issues which they prefer to avoid discussing.

Advice for students 3.1

When discussing with potential respondents whether they would be willing to participate in the research, you could prepare a brief written summary of the proposed research, and of the contribution you envisage being made by respondents. This will ensure that all respondents receive the same information, and can take a decision on the same basis.

Many research topics of necessity involve researchers in considerable travel in order to make contact with respondents for the purposes of data collection. It is often quite easy to construct potentially fascinating research questions, but which are rather impractical in terms of contacting respondents. To take a rather extreme example, suppose that you wished to conduct interviews with members of an ethnic group living in a remote part of the Amazon basin. This may sound a fascinating research topic, but you would require the considerable time and financial support to conduct the research, and also the logistical support to sustain yourself in an isolated area. The same kind of issues could well arise with the project on Syrian refugees mentioned above. Even finding the time and money to travel within the United Kingdom to interview Syrian migrants could be prohibitive.

A very important practical issue when you are planning and refining your research question is the need to gather a sufficient volume of data for writing up your thesis. Universities normally specify the required word length for a thesis, and irrespective of the size of the sample, it is essential that you have a sufficient volume of data for analysis, in order to meet the word-length requirements. There is an interesting comparison to be made here between quantitative and qualitative research studies. In a quantitative study, let us suppose that you distribute a questionnaire to a sample of 400 respondents. It is perhaps surprising but by the time you have conducted your statistical analysis, incorporating all of the numerical data from the questionnaires, you will be left with only a small number of numerical results. Moreover, these will only normally indicate levels of probability in relation to your research question, and it will be difficult to expand on these results in order to achieve the required word length of the thesis.

However, it is a very different situation with a qualitative study. Let us suppose that you only had a sample of ten respondents for a study using interview techniques. It would be perfectly possible to collect sufficient data to complete a doctoral thesis. Interview data is usually audio recorded first and then transcribed. Extracts are then used to illustrate the developing arguments in the thesis. It is thus very important that your research question and its planned methodology will generate sufficient data to support an in-depth discussion in your thesis.

When most students are planning their research question, they assume it is important to select a topic which has not, as far as they can ascertain, been previously used in a thesis or journal article. However, it is very unlikely that there will be a problem here. Even if the subject matter were the same, there would probably still be significant differences in, say, the time and location of the study, and also in the composition of the sample. In fact, there can be an advantage in selecting a subject which has been well researched before. Most research studies require you to review and analyse the previous research literature on the subject which you are investigating. If there is a broad literature, then a literature review may be easier to write. On the other hand, if you select an extremely unusual subject upon which there are relatively few publications, then it may be difficult to identify sufficient material to discuss. However, it may be more interesting and valuable to investigate a little-researched topic. When deciding on a research question, this is an issue worth bearing in mind.

Let us summarize the issues we have raised so far in choosing a research question, and then reflect on a few further matters for consideration:

- What are the aims of your research? In simple terms, what are you hoping to find out?
- How will you finance your research, in particular, the data collection process?
- Can you make the required travel arrangements in order to collect your data?
- Do you need to take time off from work or other commitments?
- In practical terms, how will you make contact with individual respondents?
- Will the data collection process involve establishing a sense of empathy with the respondents?
- How will you inform the respondents about the nature of the research, and how will you obtain their permission to take part and provide data?
- How will you identify suitable respondents?
- How will you determine a suitable sample size?
- How much previous research has been conducted in this area?

Advice for students 3.2

If you are employed and wanting to conduct research, it may be possible to collect data from colleagues at work. The practical advantages of this approach are that you would not need to travel to collect data, and your colleagues may supply you with a lot of interesting data. However, you would need to obtain the permission of line managers, and your colleagues may be slightly cautious about supplying information which might be sensitive within the organization. Respondents may also wish to remain anonymous in any accounts of the research. It would also be advantageous to read examples of similar research, and to consider some of the measures taken in terms of research ethics.

These are just some of the issues which may come to mind when you are trying to precisely define the nature of your research question. As you get closer to defining your research question, you will also need to make enquiries about a suitable person to act as your thesis supervisor. When such a person is identified, they may make further suggestions about the nature of your study, and how it should be conducted.

However, arguably the key issues in determining your research question are, first of all, to select a broad subject area, and subsequently to define the aims of the research. Engaging with this process should help you to narrow down the potential research questions and ultimately to decide upon the methodology for the study. Let us suppose that you are interested in investigating the complexities of the role of a headteacher of a large high school. You are aware of some of the more overt aspects of the job, such as staff management, conducting assemblies and organizing speech days. However, you are really interested in exploring the rather more subtle and nuanced facets of the job, with a view to constructing a picture of the hidden complexities of the role.

In the face of this broad aim for the research, you may decide that it can only be achieved through a detailed question-and-answer, or interview approach. The proposed study appears to lend itself to a qualitative methodology, and after due consideration you decide to opt for a case study approach of a single headteacher. You realize that this idea will be contingent upon identifying an individual who is prepared to give you a considerable amount of time, and also to share with you some of the more complex and normally hidden aspects of the job. The logical process in planning your research is to draw up a list of provisional aims, and to evaluate the implications of these in terms of sample size and methodology. Having checked that such issues as contact with potential respondents seems realistic, you are probably ready to try to express your research idea in the form of a provisional title.

The title for your research study will ultimately be printed on the front cover of your thesis and will provide for the potential reader the key aspects of the study. These are usually the broad subject area for the research, and an indication of the methodology used. In terms of the headteacher study, the following might be possibilities.

A fairly formal title might be:

A case study enquiry into the professional life of a high school headteacher.

It has become quite common to divide the title into two sections as follows:

The hidden life of a high school headteacher: a case study enquiry.

Other variants might be:

Discipline in a high school: A case study of the role of the headteacher.
The role of the headteacher in the enhancement of academic standards: a case study approach.

It is certainly worth investing a little bit of time and thought into a suitable title, as among other things it is the first aspect of the thesis which the potential reader comes across.

Hypothesis testing compared with inductive theorizing

It is essential in a research study to have a structured and systematic approach to the resolution of a research question. The way in which the research question is framed has a major effect upon the theoretical orientation which is most appropriate for conducting the research. For instance, if you already are interested in a particular theory or general proposition about the world, and wish to test its veracity, then a deductive approach would be more appropriate. As an example, we might propose that the educational background of parents has an influence upon the educational attainment of children. The better educated the parents, the higher the potential attainment of the children. Hence we have a general theory that there is a connection between parental education and the school performance of children. This leads us to a more specific hypothesis that the higher the educational level of parents, the higher will be the attainment of children. We would then collect some data on parental and children's attainment in order to determine whether there seems to be any evidence to support or negate this hypothesis. Upon analysing the data, we might feel that there is simply a relationship or correlation between children's and parent's education, or that, more specifically, parental education level actually causes the level of education in their children. The nature of your data, and its analysis, will affect the strength of the claim which you feel justified in making.

In *deductive theorizing*, then, there is an original theory which we wish to examine, and a hypothesis derived from that which we test in as objective a manner as possible. When we have completed this process, there is a sense in that we have a fairly clear understanding of the truth or otherwise of our original theory. This kind of approach to the acquisition of knowledge tends to be more appropriate for research where we intend to collect quantitative data, and hope to conclude our study with fairly precise statements about the research area. However, there is a very different approach to research, which does not start from a position in which we assume we know the key factors or variables at play, but within which we adopt a more open-ended, exploratory approach to the subject area. This type of research theorizing is known as induction, and is the principal concern of this book.

In *inductive reasoning* it is more a case of creating theory rather than testing it. When we have selected a broad topic for investigation, induction commences with the collection of a range of observations. Sometimes this kind of data is collected in a fairly random manner. Once collected, it is sorted and arranged in a more structured manner, so that eventually some tentative hypotheses can be created. These are then combined into a theory which is essentially provisional, and which can be adapted, depending upon its ability to predict or explain future events. Such a theory is not seen as being the final word on the subject being investigated, but rather a temporary generalization about the topic, to be adapted and refined as further evidence comes to light. As the original data collection is conducted in a rather unstructured manner, there is a more subjective approach to inductive research when compared with deductive research. In comparison with deduction, there is less of a tendency to investigate and suggest precise connections between variables, and more of an intent to try to understand the deeper relationships, meanings and connections within the social actors in the subject area.

In the case of the subject area above, concerned with parental education levels, we might start the inductive process by interviewing a sample of parents in order to explore their educational attainments, and also the ways in which they tried to help and motivate their children with their school work. Having also collected some data on the educational performance of the children, we might formulate some provisional hypotheses. These might include, for example, propositions about the availability of books in the family home, or the extent to which parents arrange educational visits and activities for their children. Ultimately these hypotheses could be combined into a provisional theory. It is also worth noting that inductive and deductive theorizing can be viewed as alternating processes or as a cyclical process. The theory which has been developed through the inductive process can subsequently be viewed as the starting point for a process of deductive theorizing. The two logical processes then proceed one after the other, with a gradual refining of the overall theory taking place.

The investigation of cultural variation

One of the principal features of contemporary society is its multi-cultural nature. After the Second World War and the demise of the European-founded colonial system, there developed a mass movement of peoples in many parts of the world which has continued to the present day. In the United Kingdom for example, this has been characterized by immigration from the Caribbean and from the Indian sub-continent in particular. In more recent times, the conflicts in the Middle East have resulted in the mass movement of migrants and refugees to Europe and then on to the United Kingdom. This phenomenon has attracted the attention of social researchers. Where the particular interest concerned such issues as the number of migrants arriving in the United Kingdom, or the number obtaining employment, then this kind of subject would lend itself to quantitative studies. On the other hand, where the research interest involved such issues as the interaction between indigenous and migrant cultures and religions, or the social pressures involved in settlement in the host country, then there is great scope here for qualitative studies.

Research involving cultural, *religious and ethnic groups* is, however, very complex, and raises issues which are not seen in other types of research. An important preliminary concern is the nature of the particular ethnic group from whom you intend to collect data. Suppose, for example, that you intend to collect data from members of the Sikh community. In terms of articulating your research question, you would probably need to decide the nature of the particular features of the Sikh community which are of interest to you. It may be, for example, that you are interested primarily in the Sikh religion, in the principal scripture, the Guru Granth Sahib, and in the cultural and religious life of the gurdwara, the main location of worship. On the other hand, you may be primarily interested in the Sikh diaspora, its initial causes, and the social consequences for Sikhs in the host countries. Finally, you might be interested in the origins of Sikhism in the Punjab area of India and Pakistan. When conducting qualitative research with such a community, it would be desirable to determine the cultural dimension which is to be the focus of the research, and to ensure that you possess at least some minimal understanding of the key features of the culture. In that way, when you are interviewing respondents, you would be able to exhibit a degree of confidence in discussing cultural matters which would hopefully encourage respondents to be forthcoming in providing in-depth data.

Case study 3.1

Let us suppose that you wish to conduct research on the religious beliefs and practices of a Thai Buddhist community. The members of the community have a very open approach to your joining their religious activities, and are very willing to answer questions about their spiritual practices. This study may well lend itself to a participant observation approach whereby you could in effect act as an 'insider', collecting data while engaging with all the normal everyday activities of the group. It might also be important to try to learn the meaning and correct pronunciation of several key scriptural terms in order to give legitimacy to your discussions with group members.

The nature of terminology can be complex when considering cultural and ethnic groups. When we speak about Sikhs, for example, there is an appreciation that we are discussing a specific religion, along with certain cultural and religious customs, such as men wearing a turban and comb to keep their uncut hair in place. There is also an understanding that we are discussing an ethnic group which originated in the Punjab, but which for historical, political and social reasons participated in a diaspora which has taken them to many different parts of the world.

In other cases, however, terminology such as 'South Asian' can be employed in research, and yet leaves some ambiguity in terms of the specific cultural groups being employed to generate samples. For example, in the geographical region to which we might approximately refer as South Asian, there may be represented several major world religions such as Hinduism, Buddhism and Islam. As religion is a major determinant of cultural norms, it would be very difficult to ignore such an important variable. In addition, when conducting qualitative research and if the researcher is trying to familiarize themselves with aspects of the culture and religion, it would be necessary to take religion into account when selecting a sample. Bhopal (2004: 441) provides an interesting discussion of terminology in relation to racial and ethnic groups.

Of course, researchers can decide to employ their own categories in relation to ethnicity, and this use of researcher definitions is more in keeping with a quantitative, positivist approach to research. The alternative, and one more appropriate in qualitative studies, is to encourage respondents to create their own definitions of ethnicity or cultures. In this way the respondent decides whether religion, geographical origins, or cultural characteristics should be the predominant feature of ethnic definition. There is also the issue that with a much greater level of ethnic interaction and integration in the world, ethnicity has become a much more varied concept. One can no longer expect rigid definitions of culture and ethnicity to remain fixed for long period of time. We have to accept a certain degree of variability in ethnicity, as society changes. It is also necessary to appreciate that research involving race and ethnicity is also potentially vulnerable to the issues of prejudice, bias and discrimination, let alone racism, which are features of some aspects of contemporary society.

Power, inequality and repression in research

We have a tendency to think of the concept 'research' as involving objective thought processes which reveal 'truth' in a balanced, dispassionate manner. Reality, however, is rather more complex than this. Let us consider for a moment, the way in which research is supported both financially and in terms of general resources. When someone has an idea for a research study, they normally will develop a written proposal, and submit it to a funding body such as a university, research council, or professional body. Such organizations will not have unlimited funds, and will need to make decisions about whether to support a proposal, based on a number of factors. A proposal may be supported, for example, because it matches established priorities of the organization, because it appears to offer good value for money, or because it will enable a number of students to work towards their doctorates. However, what is inescapable is that the academics and researchers on the selection panel have the power to decide that their organization will support one proposal and not another. In this way it can happen that certain topics or questions become the subject of more extensive research than others. It is worth noting also that research findings are sometimes used to support government policies, or to suggest new policies. In this way, some research findings may result in more practical outcomes in society.

The process of research then is not immune from the power relationships in society. Researchers may propose topics in the knowledge that they are relatively popular at the moment, and hence there may be some current support for them. Students may also be attracted to work with certain leading academics and to join their research teams as junior researchers or as respondents. This, however, also brings responsibilities for the academics.

When an academic or researcher is interviewing a respondent, or collecting other forms of qualitative, interpretive data, then it is important that the researcher remains sensitive to the differential *power relationship* between the researcher and the respondent. The researcher may be a well-known professor, and the respondent may be somewhat in awe of them. In this case it is the moral responsibility of the researcher to be sensitive to the type of questions which are asked, in terms of their not being too intrusive, or venturing into areas which may cause a degree of stress. The issue of intrusion is discussed by Dickson-Swift et al. (2007: 330). It may be the case, for example, in such areas as life history research, that the researcher inadvertently strays into aspects of childhood experience which the respondent has repressed. The raising of these issues could cause considerable anxiety for the respondent, and hence it is important that the researcher is sensitive to this possibility.

During the data collection process, it may become evident to the researcher that the perspective or world-view of the respondent diverges from that of the researcher. This should not be regarded as an inconvenience or negative feature of the research, but it may in fact be seen as a potential strength. In interpretive research there is a sense in which all perspectives are seen as potentially different but equal. In qualitative research the viewpoints of respondents all contribute to a developing theory, with no single perspective being perceived as more valid than another.

Feminist approaches to research

Feminist research is an area of practice in which the perspectives of respondents and researchers can be varied and nuanced, yet at the same time there exist common themes which speak to the female experience within society. One of the key characteristics of feminist research is that it involves subjects which address the limitations experienced by women because of either structural elements in society, or because of male values, psychology or attitudes. Typical themes for feminist research include:

- the consequences of traditional family and child-care roles in terms of establishing and developing career pathways;
- the difficulties of operating or working within male-dominated organizations, and sustaining a sense of autonomy, freedom, independence and empowerment;
- developing the confidence and ability to deal with and counteract aggressive and dominating male behaviour;
- exploring mechanisms whereby the male-dominated aspects of society can be changed, for example, in the proportion of women in senior management roles in organizations;
- processes whereby women can be empowered to assume more decision-making functions in society.

Case study 3.2

Let us suppose that you wish to investigate the informal networks among men within a large work organization. You are particularly interested in the advantages such networks provide for men in the workplace, and the way in which you believe they enhance promotion prospects. You are also interested in the relative absence of such networks among female employees. This study is, by its nature, characteristic of feminist research. It probably also would benefit from an interview approach, whereby you could interview men, possibly in a group situation, and explore their views on the potential advantages of informal networks.

One of the key features of feminist research is that it is not simply involved in the description and analysis of situations involving women in society. Feminist research not only attempts to analyse and illuminate aspects of society within which women are disempowered and unable to exercise their potential, but also it seeks to identify strategies which can be employed to transform society. Hart (2006: 41) addresses issues of power and male domination in research.

Although feminist research can legitimately employ either quantitative, qualitative or mixed methods research, there has traditionally been an antipathy to quantitative-based methods in feminist research. It has been felt by some female researchers that quantitative methods reflect a male approach to research and a male-oriented choice of research topics. Quite apart from this, there are other arguments for the use of qualitative and interpretive approaches in a feminist context. As already noted, a key feature of feminist research is to reveal and analyse areas of social life in which women are disempowered. Such aspects of life are often hidden and difficult to document. The most potent forms of data are often the personal accounts and explanations of individual women. In order to collect this type of data, methods such as interviews, ethnographies and life histories often offer the most effective approach. The data thus collected provides a more authentic picture of the lives of women, and when subjected to interpretive analysis enables researchers to accumulate a more accurate image of the interaction between women and contemporary society.

Research in the postmodern world

During the first half of the twentieth century there remained a broad belief in the value of sweeping social, psychological, philosophical and political theories which had the capacity to explain the existing world and to predict future developments. However, one of the consequences of the traumatic events of the Second World War was a considerably reduced faith in these grand theories. People began to realize that the world was significantly less predictable than previously thought. In the past there was the assumption that grand theory would enable us to understand the world, and provide us with a degree of stability. The Second World War had, however, disabused us of this notion, and a theory called *postmodernism* emerged. There is further analysis of the concept of postmodernism in Ward (2010: 4).

There developed an increasing realization that society was more accurately conceptualized as existing in a state of fluidity. No longer were there 'facts' or theories which mirrored a sense of objective truth, but rather there was a range of beliefs and propositions which existed within prevailing social and philosophical contexts. The intellectual climate gradually became one in which objective views of the world were replaced by more subjective and relativistic concepts. There was a multiplication of the number of different world-views resulting in an increasingly plural conception of society, an issue discussed by Firat and Venkatesh (1995: 240). At the centre of these developments in the latter decades of the twentieth century was the French philosopher, Jean-François Lyotard (1924–98). He used the terms meta-narratives or grand narratives to describe the kind of all-embracing philosophies which had been characteristic of the modernist period. He stressed that such systems of thought were no longer relevant in the postmodern world, and stressed the advent of the new pluralism of ideas.

It can be argued then that qualitative, interpretive approaches are more suited to a research situation where there exists a multitude of different perspectives and world-views. Respondents are encouraged to articulate their own viewpoints which are then synthesized into a provisional theory through a process of inductive theorizing.

Learning content

In this chapter you should have become familiar with the following ideas:

- deductive theorizing
- differential power between researcher and respondent
- hypothesis testing
- inductive research
- introduction to feminist research
- religious and ethnic minorities
- research and postmodernism
- selecting titles for research studies

Chapter 4

Sampling strategies in qualitative research

Chapter summary

In this chapter you will learn about the importance of sampling in all types of research, and in particular the features of sampling in qualitative methods. There is an explanation of the reasons for typically small samples in qualitative research, and for the different ways in which such samples are drawn. Finally, there is a discussion of the way in which the validity of conclusions can be enhanced when dealing with small samples.

The importance of sampling

Let us suppose that we wished to collect data on the continued professional development undertaken by nurses working in the National Health Service. One of our first steps would probably be to define what we meant by the terms 'continued professional development', and 'nurse'. It may seem rather unnecessary to define what we mean by a 'nurse', but nurses may have different levels and types of qualifications, and they may specialize in different clinical areas. In other words, one of the first steps for any researcher is to be clear about the terms used in the study, and to be able to define the parameters of the research. By 'parameter', I mean the respondents to whom the results of the research will ultimately apply. This is sometimes known as the research population.

Having defined the type of nurses who, it is hoped, will supply data for the study, the researcher has then to resolve various practical problems such as how to make contact with the respondents, and how to actually collect the data. There is also a major issue in relation to the number of nurse respondents. In order to conduct the research, you would require such information as the names and communication details of potential respondents, and assurance that they would be willing to participate. Even if you could legally access this type of information, it would remain a major problem to try to contact and collect data from all of the respondents at whom the research was aimed. There are relatively few research studies in which it is feasible to collect data from the entire research population.

The solution is to somehow select a smaller group from the population who are representative of it as a whole. In other words, as far as it is possible to ascertain, the smaller group has the same features or characteristics as the population in its entirety. The smaller group is termed a *sample*. Data is collected from the sample in the expectation that the data will be typical of the whole population. For this to be so, it is important that careful attention is given to the selection of the sample. There are many well-established procedures for the selection of samples, and these are discussed later in the chapter.

Advice for students 4.1

There is a temptation to think of the design of a research study as consisting of a series of linear stages and decisions. For example, we think of a topic, we write some aims, we decide on a methodology and sampling strategy, and then we collect and analyse some data. Although research is often presented in that way, in reality, we need to consider all of these issues simultaneously. When you are considering, for example, the type of people who may be your respondents, you also simultaneously need to reflect on whether they can provide you with sufficient suitable data.

Probability and non-probability sampling

There are many different strategies which can be employed to take samples, but it is perhaps helpful to think of these as belonging to two broad categories. First, *probability samples* are more typically associated with quantitative research and statistical analysis. In this type of sampling, we normally know the size of the sampling frame or population, and we are also aware of the individual units which make up the population. It is then possible, through a process of randomized selection, to choose a sample which we hope is typical of the overall population. In this type of random sampling every member of the total population has a known probability of being included in the final sample. If, for example, our total population has 100 members, and we would like a sample size of 20, then we use a form of randomized selection 20 times in order to create our sample. One of the traditional methods of selection was to draw names or numbers from a hat, although this has tended to be replaced by using random number tables or computer software selection. Random sampling tends to be employed in quantitative research where it is intended to analyse data using statistical techniques. Such procedures reduce or eliminate bias in the sampling process, and should enable conclusions from the sample to be generalized to the remainder of the population.

However, for all its scientific advantages and logical approach, there may be circumstances where probability sampling is not the most appropriate approach. Imagine, for example, that you want to investigate some of the causes of alcohol addiction, and for this you require a sample of alcoholics. Now it would be impossible in this case to work out the size of the total potential sample, and hence not possible to randomly sample a known percentage of the population. In addition, since many of the potential respondents would be registered with clinical organizations and hence would have their identity protected by confidentiality rules, it would be difficult to contact them. It might, however, be possible to pass on details of the proposed research programme to organizations treating alcoholics, and ask people to contact you if they were interested in taking part. You would not necessarily need to accept all of the volunteers as respondents, but could apply your own criteria. After an initial screening procedure, you might realize that some of the volunteers have more relevant experience than others in relation to the aims of your research. You could exercise your own judgement in terms of selecting potential respondents. This would be an example of *non-probability sampling*.

The resulting sample would normally be much smaller than in the case of a probability sample. In a research project such as this, you would be likely to employ qualitative methods, such as interviews or personal diaries. Non-probability sampling would offer you the opportunity to collect a great deal of in-depth and rich data from each of your respondents. Although you would not have the number of respondents as with a random sample, this could be compensated by the depth of the data obtained.

In non-probability sampling, the researcher is exercising considerable subjectivity in deciding upon members of the sample. This can be viewed as both a strength and a weakness. It does lay the research process open to suggestions of bias. However, on the other hand, it does enable the researcher to select respondents who are interested in the project, and have a relevant background to contribute to the research. It remains true that the members of the sample may not be very typical of the range of people addicted to alcohol, and therefore it may be difficult to apply the research findings on a larger scale. However, if we used a questionnaire survey approach to collect data, there would be little opportunity for respondents to express their feelings in detail. On the other hand, with a non-probability sample using a qualitative approach, the researcher should be able to explore the deeper feelings of the respondents.

Advice for students 4.2

It is worth remembering with qualitative research that you are often asking respondents to talk about some of their most intimate thoughts, and that this may at times be difficult for them. This can be a lot to ask, and during an interview or discussion you may at times need to amend your line of questioning in order to be slightly less intrusive, and perhaps more sensitive to the complexity of the issues.

Sample sizes in qualitative research

In qualitative research the size of the sample is nearly always smaller than in quantitative research. In the latter case, there is the need to have a sufficiently large sample in order to make statistical generalizations. The actual sample use will depend upon such factors as the size of the population, and the type of statistical test which is intended to be used. In qualitative research the size of the sample may be influenced by a number of factors. The aims of the research are one of these. For example, if you wish to conduct a case study, then the size of the sample will be determined partly by the number of people involved in the 'case'. At one extreme, a case study may involve a single person, or it may involve the study of a single organization which employs several hundred employees. This is not to say that your sample would consist of 50 or 60 employees. Bearing in mind that you would probably intend to collect in-depth data from your respondents, you may well be happy with a sample of 15 or 20 employees. The important issue, however, is that you are able to select respondents who have sufficient knowledge to help you investigate the topics in your research aims.

Unlike with quantitative research, there is no specific need that you should predetermine the precise number of respondents in a qualitative sample, before you commence the actual data collection. For example, if your case study is a business or commercial organization, you may commence your data collection with the most senior manager who is willing to assist with the research. Then you may continue by interviewing several middle managers, followed by other members of the workforce. You may continue sampling until a point of data saturation is reached, at which point further data collection does not appear to be revealing any further insights. A system such as this may be applicable to participant observation or ethnographic studies.

It is worth noting that in qualitative studies, not all members of the sample may be regarded as equally useful to the research study. Some respondents may give of their time very liberally, and allow you to keep returning for supplementary interviews, while others may restrict the time they give you. Different respondents will have varying degrees of knowledge and insights into the research topic, and you may decide to devote different amounts of time to separate respondents.

It is important in your thesis to be open and transparent about the reasons which resulted in your choice of respondents. Generally, the most valid reasons for the choice of respondents are those associated with the furtherance of the research aims. Almost inevitably, matters of convenience are involved in all qualitative sampling, but wherever possible it is more appropriate to base your sampling strategy on the requirements of the aims and data collection.

Purposive sampling

Purposive sampling and non-probability sampling are, to all intents and purposes, the same process. However, the term non-probability emphasizes the lack of need to create a sample which is randomized for statistical purposes, while the term purposive stresses the role of the researcher in selecting a sample which is based on the view of the researcher in structuring the data collection process. The idea of the view of the researcher provides an alternative name for purposive sampling, which is judgemental sampling.

Researchers may have a number of factors in mind when selecting a purposive sample. Suppose the research involves a study of the life of a famous politician. An important criterion for the sample members will probably be that they knew or know the politician personally, and, second, that respondents are willing to be interviewed and to provide data. The latter issue may be important since some people may be reluctant to provide data through being afraid of giving offence. It should be noted, incidentally, that a potential problem with probability sampling, is that in this example, a random sample may not select many people who know the politician, and may also select people who are unwilling to provide any detailed data.

Purposive sampling has a number of potential advantages. As it depends upon the opinion of the researcher, it can be put into practice fairly quickly, thus saving time. Researchers would decide on the criteria being sought in the respondents, and then identify appropriate people for the sample. The size of purposive samples is usually relatively small, and hence researchers can identify people not only on the basis of relevance to the research, but also in relation to ease with which they can be contacted. There are therefore potential financial savings here. A further advantage of purposive sampling is that researchers can draw upon respondents who represent extreme features or characteristics of the research topic under investigation. This is a feature of the freedom exercised by the researchers, and which enables them to explore viewpoints or attitudes at the margins of a sample. Further analysis of purposive sampling is available in Etikan et al. (2016: 2). Nevertheless, there are also disadvantages of the purposive approach which stem primarily from its subjective nature. As the decisions about sampling are taken by the researchers, there is always the danger of bias in choosing respondents. This, coupled with the intrinsically small sample sizes, makes it difficult to justify generalizing to a broader population. Overall, this means that in a thesis it is particularly important to carefully explain the basis of all the sampling decisions in order ultimately to justify the research findings.

Deviant case sampling

When we think of taking a sample for research purposes, we often consider how we could find examples which are typical of the total population. However, it is sometimes the case that atypical examples can shed light on the nature of the population. This is the essence of *deviant* case sampling. If we imagine that we want to investigate issues of patient care in hospitals, there are various approaches to sampling that we could take. For example, we could select hospitals which we believe to fairly typical in terms of standards of care, or we could select hospitals which we believe to be either very good or indeed very poor in terms of care. The advantage of taking examples which are very good or very bad is that we can try to investigate exactly why they are so good or so bad. This in itself could help us to shed light on the issues of patient care in a way which might be more difficult with more typical instances. Deviant case sampling is thus so called because it involves the selection of cases which, to one extent or another, deviate from the norm. This type of sampling is also sometimes known as extreme case sampling. It is discussed further in Draucker et al. (2007: 1144).

Deviant case sampling may be very useful as a component of a qualitative research design because it enables you to explore in depth the reasons for the sampled cases being unique or unusual. A series of probing interview questions may reveal the reasons for the sampled cases being exceptional, and this may enable you to extrapolate some of these findings to the other cases of the population.

In techniques such as deviant case sampling where there is considerable subjectivity exercised by the researcher, there is always the possibility of bias. This can be remedied to some extent by the researcher choosing outliers as examples of deviant cases, but also amended by some cases which reflect more balanced characteristics.

Case study 4.1

Let us suppose that you wanted to conduct a study of how easy it was for students to establish themselves in a career after graduating from university. Initial data collection may reveal great variation in the way that students approach this issue, and you may decide to identify respondents who were either very successful at establishing a career, or who found the situation extremely difficult. Such a deviant case sampling strategy could help you to identify more quickly the factors which are important in helping undergraduates move on to a successful career.

Stratified sampling

When you are in the process of starting your research, you may be aware that the total population with which you are concerned contains a cross-section of people with different characteristics. There may be males and females, different age groups, people who have undertaken higher education and those who have not, and people of different religious faith. Some or all of these characteristics may be important variables in your research. Let us suppose that age is one such important variable, and that you are aware that in the population as a whole, there are individuals of 30 years of age and younger, individuals aged between 31 and 50 years, and individuals aged between 51 and 70 years. These groupings or strata are not equal in size. In a perfect world, when you take your sample, there would be the same proportion of the different age strata as exist in the total population. However, if you say drew a random sample from the whole population, you would be very lucky if it contained exactly the same proportions as in the total population. However, you could solve the problem by drawing a random sample from each of the three strata, using the correct proportions from the population. By combining the three smaller samples, you would have a sample of the correct proportions.

In another example, suppose that your research involves religious faith as an important variable. In your total research population suppose there are 20 per cent Hindus, 10 per cent Sikhs and 70 per cent Christians. You may have decided that you require a sample of 50 respondents. In that case you would require 10 Hindus, 5 Sikhs and 35 Christians. These could be chosen by random selection from each of the categories or strata.

On the other hand, the three separate samples could also be selected by purposive sampling from each of the three strata. Suppose that you were also interested in the level of education completed by respondents. You might have another three strata in mind: completion of high school, completion of bachelor's degree and completion of postgraduate qualification. The additional consideration of another variable may make it more difficult to select respondents, and a purposive *stratified sampling* approach could be very useful. You could, for example, select a Hindu student with a postgraduate qualification or a Christian student with a high school leaving certificate.

Stratified sampling is, therefore, a very useful way of improving the accuracy and validity of the sampling process. In the case of randomized stratified sampling, there is the possibility of generalizing to the whole population. While this is a less-certain process with purposive stratified sampling, the latter offers a more flexible selection of respondents, which reflects the potentially wide range of respondents in the population.

Purposive stratified sampling is a useful technique for a qualitative research design, which may have the advantages of cost savings and of time savings. It enables the researcher to select precisely the respondents required, and to exercise a certain amount of flexibility in that selection. It is also important, however, to be prepared to justify the sampling process, and to offer arguments against the possibility of any selection bias.

Snowball sampling

As we have seen, the process of sampling is complex, and there are many different factors to take into account. Sometimes, however, the very subject of the research itself adds an extra dimension of complexity to the sampling process. This is particularly so where the research topic is so sensitive that potential respondents may not normally wish to admit in the public domain that they take part in the activity. This may be because the activity is socially unacceptable or illegal. There may also be an issue for respondents when they are the victims of an activity, and may not wish to discuss this. Sometimes also the research may involve people who have suffered from a particular illness or perhaps a bereavement, and may find it very difficult to discuss their feelings. There are two major concerns for the researcher here. One is the mechanism for identifying respondents and the other is the ethical issues involved in such research.

Let us take as an example, a potential research study involving leading sports stars and athletes who are gay. It may be that a good many of them may be reluctant to discuss this in any forum, because they know that many fans of the sport would be antagonistic. The normal channels of recruiting respondents may thus be difficult to operationalize. In such a case it may be possible to identify a single gay respondent, and once the data collection has been completed, to ask the respondent if they know of anyone else who might be willing to take part in the research. Once that data has been collected, the sampling proceeds in the same fashion. As it is reminiscent of rolling a snowball to collect more snow, and hence create a bigger snowball, this process is known as *snowball sampling*. The collection of respondents continues until it is difficult to attract any more, or until the data starts to become rather repetitive. Lopes et al. (1996: 1268) provide a discussion of snowball sampling in the context of a study of drug abuse.

One of the advantages of this type of sampling is that potential respondents tend to have confidence in people from their own community or who participate in the same lifestyle. They are thus sometimes more willing to join in the research. They may also have a strong interest in the research, they may have a wide knowledge of the issues involved in it, and may also have a vested interest in bringing into the public domain some of the issues which affect them and their peers.

On the other hand, some of these questions may have a negative effect on the research. The researcher is very much dependent upon the judgement of the previous respondent in identifying a new person to provide data. The previous respondent needs to have a sound grasp of the purpose of the research, and to appreciate that the ideal respondent not only is well informed about the research subject, but is able to articulate his or her views and feelings.

There are many research topics where snowball sampling may be not only useful, but also where it may be the only practical way to obtain a sample. For research on the subject of drug taking, respondents may be more inclined to participate if approached by another drug taker. On the subject of bullying, children or young people may not wish to admit that they have been bullied either in person or online. However, if approached by someone who has been bullied, they may be more likely to acquiesce. In another example, a person who is suffering from a rare and unpleasant medical condition may be willing to provide data on their experience if approached by someone who has also suffered from the illness. Snowball sampling is thus a form of sampling which may be the only realistic form of sampling in some situations. It also may demonstrate a form of empathy with the potential respondent which may encourage them to participate in the research.

Case study 4.2

If you wanted to conduct a research study concerning people who had experienced being members of a religious cult, it might be difficult to identify potential respondents. Some people may be reluctant to admit that they had been drawn into a cult, and that it reflected upon them in an adverse way. Being a member of a cult is also an activity which may involve an element of indoctrination, and it may be difficult to encourage people to be open, rational and reflective on the subject of their lifestyle. In a situation such as this, snowball sampling may be a very useful sampling option, where the first respondent may in effect act as an advocate for the research study. A further discussion of snowball sampling may be found in Oliver (2015: 48).

Key informant sampling

In snowball sampling it is very helpful if a series of well-informed participants can be identified, who can shed light on the subtleties of the research topic. The idea of identifying extremely well-informed research participants is at the heart of the sampling technique known as *key informant sampling*. Unlike snowball sampling, this type of sampling can relate to any research subject, and not simply to sensitive topics. The only requirement is that the chosen participants are able to act as 'expert witnesses'. The respondents can be selected using any method or approach. They are not chosen by using any form of randomized process, but are selected for their specialized knowledge and understanding, and for the fact that they are ideally held in high professional esteem by their colleagues. It may also help if the key informants hold different types of role or position in the particular field of research. This enables the data which they provide to be cross-checked or triangulated, thus in principle enhancing the validity of the research. The use of key informants in research in the area of health studies is discussed in Marshall (1996: 92).

Research involving the use of key informants typically employs interview research. As with most forms of qualitative research, the samples are small, and it is therefore not easy to justify creating broader generalizations from the data. Nevertheless, the depth and richness of the data collected through key informant interviews help to at least partially compensate for this drawback. In order to enhance the richness of the data it is better not to ask 'closed' questions which tend to invite short responses. Open questions invite opinions from the key informant, and also encourage them to discuss issues using their own expertise. As a result, you will often find that you make the most use of the knowledge and understanding of the respondent.

Sampling and the conclusions of the research

In the examples of sampling for qualitative research which we have discussed in this chapter, it is normal for the sample sizes to be relatively small. They can legitimately range from a sample of one, as perhaps in case study research, to 20 or 30 in interview research. There are no rigid prescriptions governing the sample size chosen, although if there is a golden rule in any research design, it is to attempt to justify each and every decision which is taken about the planning of the research programme, and the collection and analysis of the data.

Interestingly enough, the small sample sizes in qualitative research often result in very large quantities of data. The essential reason is that the data exists in verbal form. If you try recording, say, 15 minutes of interviews or dialogue, and then transcribing it into written form, you will realize immediately the quantity of data which is generated. Therefore, once you have designed your research and obtained a commitment from respondents to take part, qualitative research can be conducted relatively rapidly. The raw data can be stored safely until you have time to transcribe it, and then proceed with the analysis. Despite these major advantages it is never easy to justify the making of generalizations from small-scale qualitative research. Let us now examine some of the arguments which can be useful in helping to achieve this end.

The essential problem with the analysis of this type of data is that the process can seem to be subjective. In order to counteract this, researchers have a number of possible measures at their disposal. One possibility is to survey relevant and connected literature in order to determine whether other researchers have drawn similar conclusions. This could contribute towards a feeling of confidence in your own analysis. Alternatively, researchers can carefully examine their data to ascertain whether there are other ways of interpreting it. You could also seek among your data for alternative types of interpretation. The identification of different possible forms of interpretation does not necessarily run contrary to your own analysis, but demonstrates a measure of rigour in your analysis.

Another possible way of enhancing the rigour of your analysis is to develop self-reflective accounts of how you went about your research. By documenting such processes, you are able to open up to scrutiny your methods and to enable colleagues to judge whether they would adopt the same form of analyses. Finally, it would be valuable to include in such accounts the reasons for your selecting certain elements of your total data for analysis. Again, this would enable your peers to comment upon whether they would have selected the same data elements, or perhaps concentrated upon other aspects.

Learning content

In this chapter you should have become familiar with the following ideas:

- deviant case sampling
- generalizing from small samples
- key informant sampling
- non-probability sampling
- probability sampling
- purposive sampling
- reasons for sampling
- sample sizes in qualitative research
- snowball sampling
- stratified sampling

Chapter 5

Research ethics

Chapter summary

This chapter starts with a discussion of the way in which research and ethical questions are interconnected. It examines ways in which human dignity may be compromised if due care is not given to ethical principles. The notion of informed consent is one of the most important of these principles, and the applicability of this is analysed carefully. A number of other aspects of current research ethics practice, such as anonymity, confidentiality and the obtaining of permissions are also discussed in detail.

The relationship between ethics and research

Research is a collaborative activity. As students and researchers, we need the help of other people to give us background information about the research context, to help us identify suitable respondents, to provide us with data, and if necessary to help us with the analysis of that data. We, therefore, have an obligation to consider the effects of the research, not only upon ourselves, but upon this potentially very wide cross-section of people. The consequences of being involved in research, whether as researchers or respondents, can include feelings and opinions being passed into the public domain, adverse effects on the psychological welfare of people, and people being asked to discuss issues with which they do not feel comfortable. Therefore, research as an activity has a number of important ethical dimensions, and it is important that researchers carefully consider not only the possible consequences for themselves, but also for respondents and others. See Long and Johnson (2007: 2), for further discussion on research and ethics.

Case study 5.1

Let us suppose that you want to conduct a research study of the political and personal philosophy of a well-known politician, who is now deceased. Your preliminary investigations show that there is a great deal of documentary data available, in relation to his political activity. You are aware that he had a colourful private life, and his existing relatives could in principle provide a lot of data. However, some relatives strongly oppose publicizing his private life, and have refused to be interviewed. You are concerned about the ethics of giving unnecessary offence to relatives and wonder how to proceed.

Among a range of possible approaches, you could do one of the following:

- Adhere to a documentary research approach, and restrict yourself largely to his political career.
- Adopt a combination of documentary and interview research, but try to place limited attention on his private life.
- Use documentary and interview research, but do not exclude material as long as there is carefully triangulated evidence of its existence.

It is also potentially possible to limit the circulation of a thesis for a period of time, if there are compelling reasons so to do.

One way in which researchers can seek to justify research is to point to the potentially beneficial outcomes which may emerge from research. These may appear relatively straightforward in the case of research into dangerous clinical conditions, or into helping people avoid the impact of disease and illness. In some cases, however, a researcher may need to explain the possible benefits of a research programme rather more carefully to potential respondents in order to encourage them to participate. In the case of social science research, for example, the potential benefits may seem a little obscure to the non-academic respondent, and it may take a very careful explanation to convince potential respondents to take part.

A very important question of debate in research ethics is whether the potential results of a research programme justify the methods used to collect the data. To put this briefly, there is the question of whether the end justifies the means. For example, if the process of conducting the research involves inconvenience, discomfort, or a variety of risks, then it may seem too much to ask to try to persuade people to participate. There is also the issue of the extent to which participants fully appreciate the possible consequences of taking part in the research.

When people are invited to take part in a research project, they may not be aware of some of the conventions and procedures of working within a higher education context. They may not be aware of some of the terms used to describe the research, and this may result in their being perhaps a little too over-compliant with the demands of being a respondent. Let us look now at some of the more specific issues concerning ethics and research.

Access and permissions

Research does not exist in a vacuum. It involves interaction with organizations and with the many different types of people who have access to data. These organizations and people have a moral right, and often a legal right, to be consulted, if they are going to be asked to provide data of any kind. Let us consider some examples.

If you hope to collect data from a member of staff in an organization, such as a building society, an insurance company, a supermarket or a travel company, it is unlikely you will be able to just walk into the building and to talk to someone. You will probably need to prepare a letter of introduction, detailing the nature of the data you would like to collect, the methods you hope to use, the time it will take and how the data will be used. Your letter may well be read initially by a member of the administrative staff, who will decide to whom it will be forwarded. This person acts as a kind of buffer for the wide range of correspondence received, and is sometimes known as a gatekeeper. You may need to engage in several exchanges or letters or emails, before there is a final agreement about how to proceed. The prospective respondent may well wish to know the kind of questions which will be asked, and in particular the way in which the data will be used. In terms of the latter issue, it may be your intention to publish journal articles or a book based upon your thesis. These would probably find a wider readership than an academic thesis, and as a result your respondents may wish to exclude some topics from the interviews, and will also be possibly more cautious about what they say. In addition, your respondents may feel that they wish to have some sort of written agreement with you, which provides details of how the data collection process will proceed, and how the data will be used. You may also need to indicate how any unused data will be disposed of securely.

Increasingly, people who work within organizations are themselves becoming part-time researchers, collecting data on situations at their workplace. This may be because, as part of their staff development programme, they are studying for a higher degree. Alternatively, they may be conducting research as part of an effort to improve work-based practice. The role of teacher-researchers is a case in point. While continuing with their normal teaching role, teachers may conduct research on a new curriculum development, on the effect of new teaching resources, or on the effects of a new management style in their school or college. One of the advantages of such professionally-based research is that the teacher-researcher has relatively easy access to a sample of teachers and students. On the other hand, it will be important to seek appropriate permissions from the institutional management. This may be particularly important in the case of students, where, depending upon their age, it may be necessary to seek the permission of parents, classroom teachers or school or college principals.

Advice for students 5.1

When you are designing your research, it may well be that as part of the process of seeking permissions, you will receive advice on who should be consulted before commencing data collection. Not only is it important to respond to this advice, but you should also document this consultative process in your thesis. It demonstrates that you have consulted widely, and done your best to respond to the ethical issues implicit in your study.

The function of ethics committees

It is an indication of the growing importance of ethical issues in the conduct of research, that increasingly researchers and academics are being required to submit their research proposals for peer review. Universities are now typically setting up standing ethics committees to do this. The committees are composed of experienced researchers, and would normally consider proposals for research degrees, as well as bids for funded research programmes. It has almost become a requirement that researchers are able to confirm that their proposal has been submitted to an ethics committee, and the recommendations implemented. An ethics committee may well be interested in a range of questions including:

- whether potential respondents had been fully briefed on the nature of the research;
- whether respondents could leave the research programme easily if they felt uncomfortable about participation;
- whether data was held securely; and whether arrangements had been made to ensure the anonymity of respondents.

Ethics committees also have to address contemporary issues, such as ethical concerns involved in social media research (see Hibbin et al., 2018: 152).

It is worth noting that ethical issues in general are extremely complex and it is often not possible to reach an absolute decision about what is and is not, acceptable in terms of practice. However, this does not mean that ethics committees do not serve a useful function. The very fact that a research proposal is submitted for peer evaluation and critique is very important. It is part of a philosophy of transparency, which exposes the researcher to public examination and scrutiny.

Implicit in this process is also an element of protection for those involved in the research. The ethics committee is first of all considering the situation of the respondents and making sure in its own mind that they are not vulnerable in any way, and that all reasonable steps have been taken to protect their interests. In addition, the committee is concerned about the researchers, and wants to reasonably ensure that they are not acting in such a way as to adversely affect their careers. Finally, the committee is concerned about the institution of which it is a part, and wants to satisfy itself that any research conducted under its auspices has been carefully considered and evaluated.

In terms of protecting the interests of respondents, there are a variety of factors which a research committee may wish to consider. The age of respondents is important. The younger a respondent, the greater is the danger that they will not fully understand the implications of participating in the research. The education level of respondents is another factor which may influence the degree of understanding of the research proposal. Finally, other factors include whether, for example, there are respondents whose mother tongue is not English, and hence they may not be able to appreciate the nuances of the research proposal and what is expected of them.

Respect for human dignity

It is sometimes worth standing back and reflecting on the relative advantages of doing research, between respondents and researchers. The latter have a considerable amount to gain. They are usually either enrolled for a research degree such as a doctorate, or intent upon publishing academic journal articles. Both of these will enhance their CVs and help them further their careers. If they are employed as university lecturers, then being an active researcher, in addition to teaching, will almost certainly be a contractual commitment.

Respondents, on the other hand, have very little to gain. They may find it interesting to be involved in research, and even more so if they are interested in the topic. However, respondents do not have the same potential benefits as do the research community. Neither is it particularly common for respondents to be paid for providing data. They may receive travel expenses, but receiving an actual financial remuneration is more rare. The reason for mentioning this distinction is that it reminds us of the considerable contribution made by respondents, without there being any tangible benefits. It reminds us as researchers must always try to treat respondents in a dignified way, bearing in mind the considerable help we receive from them. The concept of dignity is analysed by Edlund et al. (2013: 852).

To take a more everyday, practical example, imagine a research study on homelessness, where you as the researcher manage to enlist the help of a small sample of homeless people, who sleep in a hostel at night, and spend their days wandering around a city center. You arrange to conduct a series of interviews with the respondents, and inevitably start to get to know them, buying them coffees and snacks. You meet different members of the group, on a regular basis, several times a week. You gradually become a significant part of their lives. It is fairly clear that they look forward to meeting you, not simply because of the food you buy for them, but also because you represent an element of contact with the 'real' world outside their rather limited horizons. In addition, they also learn about your life, which also has the effect of broadening their perspectives on the world. However, after about six months of collecting interview data, there comes the time when you realize you have quite sufficient data for your thesis. You no longer need the respondents, but you are aware that they have come to depend on you. You do not feel that you can continue with the relationship, and yet you are unsure how you can end it with dignity. You do not feel it is fair to simply walk away, yet on the other hand, you feel it would be very awkward to have a protracted and gradual ending of the connection.

There is no easy answer to this problem of how to disengage from a research relationship. Perhaps the best strategy is to be aware of the existence of the problem when you first start the research, and to do your best to explain to the respondents that the relationship will be temporary. There is no ideal solution to this problem, but an initial explanation along these lines is probably the best we can do to help preserve the *dignity* of those who help us with our research.

Anonymity and confidentiality

When researchers are discussing a proposed research project with potential respondents, or when respondents are asking questions about a project, one of the commonest issues raised is whether the identity of people will be hidden, and also who will have access to the final research report. In other words, people are interested in the issues of *anonymity* and *confidentiality*.

Participants are interested in anonymity for a number of reasons. They often wish to be reassured that the views which they express will not be attributed to them. During the research process, participants will sometimes express very personal views on sensitive topics, and they may not wish to be associated with those views in the public domain. If they are not confident about their anonymity in the final thesis or research report, they may feel somewhat inhibited in terms of making comments. In a sense, respondents can feel liberated by assurances of anonymity, for they can then feel more free to express their opinions.

There are a variety of ways in which you can disguise the identity of respondents in your final thesis or article. One of the most popular is the use of fictional names when you are attributing the source of extracts from interview transcripts. As you are writing your thesis and including extracts from diaries, interviews or focus groups, you need to note the fictional name of the respondent, and on a separate sheet of paper, the real name. You will then have an accurate record of the identities of all the respondents whose data you have used. It may be worth noting that when you select fictional names for respondents you will need to select appropriate ones in relation to such variables as gender and ethnicity. If, for example, you need to select specifically male or female names for respondents from different cultures, then you may need to obtain specialist linguistic advice. Some researchers prefer to use letters or numbers to preserve the anonymity of respondents. This works perfectly well, although it can interfere somewhat with the language style of the finished text when it is being read.

No matter how careful you are with the use of fictional names, it is rarely possible to absolutely guarantee anonymity. For example, suppose you have been interviewing staff in a large manufacturing company. In your thesis you may not refer to the company by name, but may say that it is located in a

northern suburb of a specified city. Knowing the nature of the products manu-
factured, a reader of your thesis may be able to make a reasonable guess as to
the identity of the company. In addition, if you note that you interviewed the
Head of IT, and also the chief finance officer, then if a reader wanted to identify
these people, it would not be too difficult. It is thus doubtful whether it is possible to give absolute assurances of anonymity. However, the very fact that as a
researcher you have done your best to achieve this is a positive acknowledge-
ment of the importance of research ethics.

The subject of confidentiality is related to anonymity in the sense that both
terms are connected to the concept of privacy, but there are significant differences. The idea of a research thesis being confidential, is a statement that when
the thesis is completed, it will have a limited circulation and readership. This
may be something which is desired by the respondents and perhaps also by the
researcher. The fact that some people would like to limit the circulation of the
thesis is usually a feature of the nature of the subject matter of the research.
The complexities of confidentiality are considered by Wiles et al. (2008: 419).

It is not sufficient to claim that a research thesis will be confidential, but
rather you should also say to whom it will be confidential. Clearly it will be read
by those academics authorized by the university to examine it. In addition,
once the examination process has been satisfactorily completed, the thesis is
usually placed in the university library, and may also be available on-line. This
means that, in principle, it can be viewed by a wide range of people. Thus,
before a research project commences, and during discussions with potential
respondents, it would be good practice to explain both the system for trying to
assure anonymity, and also the extent to which the final thesis will have a
degree of confidentiality.

Informed consent

As the previous section suggests, it is important from an ethical point of view to
be open and transparent with respondents about the nature of the research project you are about to undertake. This can be summed up by the term '*informed
consent*', which is one of the most important principles of research ethics. As the
name of the term implies, when you are asking people to take part in your
research in any capacity it is important from an ethical perspective to ensure
that they are fully informed about the project before they give their consent. It
is very easy when you are full of enthusiasm about the research, to give a quick
summary, and then ask people to become interviewees or participants. However, this is not really fair, as people may later regret their involvement.

Let us first consider what we mean by 'informed' consent. Potential participants should be given all of the information which they could possibly need in
order to decide whether or not they wish to participate. They should be informed
as to their precise role in the research, and in particular the way in which they
will be asked to provide data. They should be given examples of the kinds of

question they will be asked, and the manner in which the data will be recorded. It would be very helpful for them to know some practical details about the data collection such as where the process will take place; how long it will last and whether there will be several sessions of interviews. One of the first things which will occur to potential respondents is probably how they will fit this commitment into their lives. If they are going to be expected to undertake travel commitments, they may very well ask if they will be remunerated for this. Overall, then, respondents should be given as much initial information as possible before you ask them to agree to take part. Even then, it is good practice to emphasize that if they change their mind during the research, then they are completely free to withdraw from the project. This is important for their own peace of mind, and may well help them feel more relaxed during the research project. In addition, in relation to the discussions in the previous section, it will be important to mention the steps you have taken with regard to anonymity and confidentiality.

It may be useful to summarize the key points of the research in a short leaflet for distribution to potential respondents. Although this will not entirely replace a verbal description, it will ensure that all respondents receive the same basic information about the research. You can also repeat the principle that people can withdraw from the research if they feel at all unhappy about any elements of the process. In terms of giving consent to take part in the research, you could simply ask for the verbal agreement of respondents, or alternatively provide space on the form for them to provide a signed agreement. (See Bowman et al., 2012: 32, for further discussion of informed consent.)

Research involving vulnerable people

Sometimes, irrespective of all the best efforts of the researcher to put in place the principles of informed consent, the prospective participants may find it difficult to understand the exact nature of the research. Hence they are not sufficiently well informed to be able to make a decision about giving or withholding their consent.

There may be many different reasons for this. Some respondents may not have pursued their education to a level where they can fully comprehend the nature of research. They may not understand its purpose; they may have great difficulty understanding the specialist sociological and philosophical terminology; and they may not be able to appreciate the more technical elements of the way in which the data is to be collected. When the problem is of this nature, one possible solution is to enlist the help of a specialist study skills tutor who can simplify the explanation of the research project to some extent. This may enable the respondents to form a considered judgement about participating in the research.

A related issue concerns a situation where respondents need to possess considerable computer skills in order to provide data or to read material relevant to the research. If respondents have difficulty with these tasks, then it can affect their ability to participate. A researcher would need to take this issue into account either in terms of selecting respondents with the appropriate skills, or in providing computer training.

A good deal of research, particularly in the sphere of education, involves the collection of data from children. This is an important area of research for a number of reasons. When government is considering changes in educational policy there is often a need for research to analyse the viability of such policy changes. These changes may be in the areas of new curricula, of new approaches to teaching, or of new strategies for evaluating pupil progress. School pupils are not able to give their fully informed consent in such situations because of their age, yet it may still be possible to provide them with a brief explanation of what they are being asked to do. Normally there would be discussions with teachers and school principals, and with parents, in order to ensure that all relevant parties are informed about the proposed research and give their approval to it being carried out.

There are many other categories of people who may be regarded as vulnerable in terms of being involved in the research process. In broad terms, people with social or psychological difficulties may not be completely able to give their informed consent. Such people may include those who are homeless, those who are suffering from depression or social exclusion, and those engaged in addictive patterns of behaviour. On the one hand, research into the lifestyles of such groups may be very important in terms of helping them; on the other, it is important for researchers to be sensitive to the implicit ethical issues of such research.

In all research situations involving potentially vulnerable respondents, peer review through a research ethics committee is one of the best approaches to try to ensure that the needs of respondents are taken into account. The varied expertise of such a committee helps to decide when it might be advisable not to continue with a research project, or at least to provide limits to the data collection. Ethical issues are among the most complex concerns addressed in research. That very complexity may mean that it is rarely possible to reach definitive conclusions about ethical acceptability, but the peer review process often does help researchers to reach a degree of consensus. Ethical issues when working with vulnerable people are discussed in Tee and Lathlean (2004: 537).

Beneficence and non-maleficence

So complex are ethical issues in research that it is very often useful to adopt philosophical principles which assist us in taking decisions. The principles of *beneficence* and *non-maleficence* are such philosophical concepts. Beneficence is the principle that, when conducting research, we should be governed by the desire to do good to others, or to have a benign influence on the world. Hence, when selecting a research topic, we should try to select one whose outcome will hopefully improve the lot of other people. In addition, when actually conducting the research, we should try to select strategies which will have a beneficial effect upon people. In life history research, for instance, there may often be opportunities to encourage respondents to reflect upon their lives, and to take positive decisions about the future.

Case study 5.2

One of the issues about adopting philosophical principles such as beneficence is that in order to apply them effectively, one has to be very precise about their use. We may feel that conducting research in order to do good to others is sufficiently clear, but in philosophical terms it depends on what we mean by 'good'. Suppose you wish to conduct an ethnographic study of a cultural group who live in a fairly isolated part of Australia; you may feel that it will be a positive effect to help them adjust better to a modern technological society. However, a different perspective would be to suggest that the research process may erode valuable elements of their traditional culture. In order then to proceed with an ethnographic study in keeping with the concept of beneficence, you would need to carefully define the concept of beneficence in this particular context. This analysis would also be an important part of the discussion of research ethics in your thesis.

In the case of non-maleficence, the philosophical emphasis is upon not doing anything which might cause harm to others. Of course, this is not necessarily easy since one may try to increase the sum total of good in the world, but inadvertently cause harm. Again, one might take the case of life history research. During a life history interview, one might decide to try to avoid discussion of issues which could cause psychological distress to respondents. This may not always be easy to do, but at least it provides a positive principle to work by. This is the fundamental benefit of concepts such as beneficence and non-maleficence. They provide principles which are aspirational in the context of research, and which have the capacity to produce positive outcomes.

Covert research

As we have discussed, one of the most important principles of research ethics is that of informed consent. This principle emphasizes the importance of openness and transparency when conducting research, and of trying to ensure that respondents fully understand all elements of the research project in which they are involved. However, there may be circumstances or types of research during which it may be unnecessary to be continually reminding participants that what they have just said may be used as research data. Let us suppose that you are conducting research on the social relationships which exist in a sports club of which you are a member. You make arrangements to conduct some interviews with key members of the club, and you anticipate that this data, when transcribed from recordings, will constitute the main part of the research. However, during many informal situations in the club you come across several elements of conversation and interaction which would be very useful as data. You also feel that it would create an unnatural situation at the club if you were frequently asking people if they minded you using a brief piece of conversation as data. The club members already know that you are conducting research, and to be continually reiterating this might, you feel, create an artificial situation. In fact, it could be argued that this very artificiality may affect what we might term the social ecology of the research setting, and hence change the research environment.

Of course, technically speaking, if you do not fully inform respondents about your actions, it could be said that you are conducting research in a *covert* manner, and hence acting unethically. There are other similar situations in which, for example, you might observe some aspects of human behaviour and wish to use it as research data, say, some illegal act. It is possible to take an absolute view about such situations, and decide never to use data which has been collected informally and covertly. On the other hand, one might adopt a more relativistic position in which one takes situations as they arise and tries to assume a 'common-sense' position, doing one's best to resolve ethical dilemmas as they occur.

Advice for students 5.2

The process of writing a thesis could be regarded as a process of laying bare your entire reasoning and thought process for your research. You will be confronted by many complex ethical situations and difficult decisions, where there do not seem to be clear-cut answers. As you write your thesis you should try to discuss this complexity and illuminate the decision-making process which you have adopted. This will help create a much more sophisticated thesis, and demonstrate to examiners the depth of your analysis.

Having said all of this, however, one is perhaps left with the view that we should normally regard any form of covert research as, in principle, unethical, albeit with the caveat that there may be a number of situations which should be decided on their own merits.

Learning content

In this chapter you should have become familiar with the following ideas:

- anonymity
- beneficence

- confidentiality
- covert research
- human dignity
- informed consent
- non-maleficence
- permissions in research
- role of research ethics committees

Part  III

The methods of collecting qualitative data

Part III

The methods of collecting
qualitative data

Chapter 6

Research questions and plans for methodology

> **Chapter summary**
> The structure of a research project includes the plans for the conduct of the research, the anticipated data collection methods, and the procedures for the data analysis. The chapter starts by considering the proposed research question, and the implications of this for data collection and analysis. It is important that all aspects of the research design fit together as a coherent whole, and this chapter will reflect this necessity.

The nature of the research question

Perhaps the first essential of a good thesis is to have a clear concept in one's mind of the broad purposes of the research. Much social science research has as its intention the making of general statements about the world which can be shown to be applicable in a wide range of situations. This is not easy to accomplish since most individual social contexts are very complex with a wide range of variables and factors which influence that context.

For example, we might consider a research topic such as that of social exclusion. You might decide to research this topic, and in particular the factors which cause people to feel excluded from the main opportunities and possibilities in life. You may decide that this subject would be suitable for a qualitative, interpretive study, partly because you cannot pre-determine the factors which might result in social exclusion, and therefore need to collect a range of empirical data in order to begin to appreciate the factors involved.

An analysis of previous research may suggest to you that factors such as a lack of educational opportunities and difficulty in taking advantage of such educational opportunities as were available, are factors in exclusion.

Nevertheless, other factors such as low income, inadequate housing, poor nutrition and lack of social opportunities, may all be elements in a highly complex network of factors which are influential in creating social exclusion. You may also be conscious that this is unlikely to be an exclusive list of factors, and the advantage of an interpretive qualitative study is that it could hopefully reveal other factors which may illuminate the issue.

The ultimate goal of the research would be to identify the most important factor or factors which influence social exclusion. This would then enable policy-makers to develop strategies to ameliorate the situation.

A qualitative approach to this topic would be useful because it would open the possibility of identifying factors which may not be evident from an analysis of existing literature or previous research, or from *a priori* analysis. The result would potentially be a generalizable picture of the key factors in social exclusion, along with a picture of the network of supporting factors.

The end result would be a theory, or series of interconnected statements, which could be applied to a wide range of social situations, and could help in improving opportunities for people. Theories developed through the process of induction do not necessarily remain unchanged for a long period. Other researchers continue to collect data on the theme of the theory, in order to establish whether the new data will be in harmony with the theory. If in fact this is so, then the theory is supported or validated, and continues to be accepted as a valid statement of relationships between the various relevant *variables*. If, on the other hand, substantial elements of the new data are not congruent with the original theory, then we can speak of the theory as having been falsified. The theory will then be adapted in the light of the new data. Subsequently other researchers will collect further data and compare this with the revised theory. The latter will then either be supported or falsified, and the cycle of validation, *falsification* or revision will continue as before.

Within a qualitative perspective then, there is no absolute and final understanding of the social world. Having created a theory of the way in which we understand a particular social issue such as exclusion, we then subject that theoretical model to continual tests in order to evaluate its effectiveness in explaining the social world. We may reach a situation in which we feel we can go no further in terms of validating the theory, and at that point we provisionally accept our theory as the best explanation of the social world which we have available. One of the tests to which we subject our theory is that we compare it with theories which have been developed by other researchers. If we find a sense of congruity between our theory and those of others, then that gives us confidence in our understanding of the world. If, however, there are differences between the various theories, then we have to be prepared to adapt and revise our theoretical understandings. Eventually we will reach a situation where we feel we can go no further for the moment. This process of developing theory through continual revision and comparison with other understandings of the world is known as *social constructionism* or *constructionism*. For social constructionists, there exists a continual process of negotiation about the world which results in an ever-changing creation of social understanding. Not only is this process a view of the mechanism by which social theory develops, but it also affects the way in which we determine the themes and questions deemed worthy of investigating through research. In other words, the nature of research questions is also a social construction. We decide to investigate those topics which emerge from our interactions with other social actors as being significant.

Advice for students 6.1

When you are conducting research for a thesis, there comes a time when you have to draw your data analysis and theorizing to a close. This point is often limited by the length of the thesis in the university regulations. With qualitative research, there is often no clear and precise end to the research. It is important, however, that you do not simply stop the research process with no explanation. It provides a much more satisfactory sense of completion for the thesis, to elaborate on the factors which have caused you to end the research at this point, and then to indicate ways in which the research could be continued.

Precision of statement of the question

The precise research questions which you have in mind are not normally articulated in the title of a thesis. The title normally states succinctly the sphere of the research, such as 'social exclusion', 'youth unemployment' or 'social care'. It also normally states the main method of investigation such as 'a case study approach', or 'an interpretive study of …'. It may also state the context of the research, such as 'an ethnographic study of adult retraining in a former mining community in the north of England'. The title is really intended to provide a succinct guide to the subject of the thesis so that a potential reader can determine quickly whether it is relevant to their own research. It is only in the *research aims* that the researcher articulates clearly and precisely the purposes of the investigation. In a qualitative study perhaps the most central aim will be the generation of a theory which will be subject to verification, as mentioned above. This intention to generate social theory could be expressed in a variety of ways. For example, you could write that the research aims to do the following:

1 Create a theoretical understanding of the subject of social exclusion in a working-class industrial context.
2 Generate a social theory which explains the problem of social exclusion in a working-class environment.
3 Theorize the phenomenon of social exclusion in order to predict how it may best be minimized in the future.
4 Construct a theory of social exclusion in order to generalize the findings to other forms of social disadvantage.

5   Provide a theory of social exclusion in order to understand the origins of the phenomenon and how best to ameliorate it.
6   Describe the impact which social exclusion has on the lives of young people in a working-class community.

There are thus many permutations of the aims of a research study. They should, however, be expressed with sufficient clarity that a reader of the thesis can appreciate from the beginning what the researcher intends to achieve.

Aims should also be measurable. That is, it should be evident what your thesis needs to achieve in order to make it clear that you have done what you said you would do at the beginning of the thesis.

It is also very important to bear in mind what you are expected to achieve in your thesis in terms of the expectations of your examiners. For example, you may state in one of your aims that you intend to 'describe a phenomenon'. This may be acceptable as an aim for a final-year undergraduate study, or possibly as part of a Master's thesis, but it is unlikely to be satisfactory for a doctoral thesis. In the latter case, one of the key requirements is that the thesis should make a significant contribution to knowledge. In order to achieve this, then an aim would be better expressed as 'to analyse the concept of …'. In other words, 'analyse' would be seen as a higher-order process than 'describe'.

Advice for students 6.2

When you are planning your research aims, it is often a good idea to read the assessment criteria for the level of thesis on which you are working. Assessment criteria for different academic levels of thesis are usually available in the university regulations. By reading these carefully and discussing them with your supervisor, you should be able to frame your aims in an appropriate way.

It is thus important to select aims which are precisely expressed, and which are achievable within the scope of your planned research. One aim which may be very important in a qualitative study is to investigate and analyse the various factors which may influence a concept such as social exclusion. We often refer to such factors as 'variables'.

The apparent variables

In qualitative research we often do not know the nature of the variables which affect a particular phenomenon. One of the key functions of qualitative research is to identify the range of variables which interact to influence the topic being researched. There are many different types of variables such as age, postcode of residence, or height. These variables are capable of being precisely measured. On the other hand, there are variables such as motivation, empathy or enthusiasm which appear rather more vague, and are apparently much more difficult to measure. The latter variables are more typical of qualitative research.

During the qualitative research process, attempts are made to clarify potential variables from the wide range of data provided by respondents. Many potential variables may be identified, but certainly in the early stages of the research, it will probably be difficult to determine which might be the most significant. One of the principal purposes of identifying variables in qualitative research is to determine the meaning which might be attributed to them by the respondents. Researchers may also try to identify situations where, when one variable changes in magnitude, another variable also changes either by increasing or decreasing. Such a situation is known as a *correlation*. It may also be possible to identify a situation where a change in one variable appears to directly result in a change in another one. Where such a relationship can be identified, it is termed a *causal connection*. Generally speaking, however, correlation and causality are difficult to demonstrate definitively in qualitative research, because the latter tends to identify variables which are not easily measurable with precision.

Theoretical basis of the research

It is possible to collect a range of qualitative data, to analyse it and then draw legitimate and meaningful conclusions, without using theoretical concepts to further the process. However, it is usually considered desirable, particularly at postgraduate level, to collect and analyse your data using a range of theoretical concepts, often derived from a wide variety of previous research studies. The concepts employed may refer to methods of collecting data, such as informal interview data, or to methods of analysis, such as interpretive approaches.

The theoretical concepts used act as a guide for you as the researcher, and also as guidance for the reader or examiner of the thesis, in that the concepts provide a framework within which the thesis can be written and understood. Besides the term '*theoretical framework*', other concepts can be used to refer to the framework within which a research study is constructed. Some researchers refer to the use of a '*theoretical perspective*' and others to a '*theoretical paradigm*'. These terms have in common the idea that they link together a range of individual concepts which can be used to understand and analyse data. It is, however, helpful that having chosen a specific term to use, you explain to the reader of your thesis the specific reasons for the selection of the term and the manner in which it is being used. This will minimize any potential confusion in the choice and use of the term.

Strategies for collecting data

Qualitative research incorporates a wide range of data collection methods, all of which are linked by the fact that the data is in the form of words. As words take up much more space in comparison with numerical data, one of the key problems with qualitative data is to distil it into a condensed but still meaningful form. Of all the varieties of qualitative data, the interview is probably the most common. It is also a type of data collection which exists in a number of different forms. Interview research can sometimes exist as a type of structured questionnaire where the researcher reads out a series of pre-determined questions, and either writes notes on, or records the responses. The notes are later presented in a more systematic form, or the recordings are transcribed. This technique is similar to a conventional written questionnaire where respondents write their responses to pre-determined questions.

Case study 6.1

Suppose you are conducting research on 'Student perceptions of first-year undergraduate life'. If as researcher you are fairly confident of the kind of issues which you would like to investigate, then you might decide to employ a structured interview which combines 'closed' questions with the opportunity for the respondent to add informal comments after each question. After each question you could ask the respondent 'Do you have any comments you would like to make on this issue?'

Here are several examples of 'closed' questions appropriate for a more formal interview:

- Are you studying all of the modules you expected to study?
- How many clubs or societies did you join in your first term?
- How many times in the first month did you see your personal tutor?
- Have you registered at the University Health Centre?
- How many lectures have you missed so far this term?

The more usual form of interview, however, is where the interviewer has a series of informal, open-ended questions which are used as prompts to initiate discussions on the topic of the research.

Case study 6.2

On the previous topic of investigating undergraduate life, here are some sample questions for a more informal interview, which employs open-ended questions. The respondent is provided with a topic and asked to respond generally to the issue. The respondent is, in a sense, much more in command of the interview interaction:

- Did you have any concerns before arriving at university for Fresher's Week?
- How easy was it to make friends?
- Did you go to many social events?
- Did you miss family and friends at home?
- What kind of help did you get from your tutor?

In interview research there is a form of continuum from structured interviews where the researcher determines the main aspects of the questions and controls much of the facets of the discussion, to informal interviews where the researcher provides only brief stimuli in order to initiate open-ended discussion. In general, however, the raw data during all types of interview research will consist of recordings of the verbal exchanges followed by the verbatim *transcription* of the recordings. Poland (1995: 293) discusses issues involved in accurate transcription. These transcripts are usually extremely lengthy, and the next stage is to read and re-read them in order to identify the principal threads of the discussion, and also to determine which sections should be incorporated into the actual thesis. This identification of key sections is an important element because it raises questions of why one section and not another has been selected by the interviewer. It is here that someone reading the thesis may raise questions of potential bias. In this context it is often a good idea for the researcher to write a *reflexive or reflective account,* which, in effect, outlines some features of the world-view or personal paradigm of the researcher, which helps to explain the significance which the researcher attaches to certain parts of the raw data. The relevance of reflexive accounts is discussed by Palaganas et al. (2017: 429).

A reflexive account is also very useful in many aspects of qualitative research, particularly in ethnographic studies. In any form of research where the researcher is in a position of proximity to a group of respondents, it is important to try to outline the thought process of the researcher in terms of giving priority to one aspect of the raw data, and not to another.

Just as it is important to try to understand potential bias in qualitative research, it is also essential to appreciate that respondents may not behave naturally when in the presence of a researcher. In other words, researchers, because of their very presence, may cause changes in the actions, behaviour and responses of the respondents. This can have an impact upon the validity of data, and this is an important issue throughout all forms of qualitative research. This phenomenon is termed *reactivity,* in a sense because it reflects the reaction of respondents to the researcher. It is particularly notable in research involving participant observation. Lietz and Zayas (2010: 191) discuss the nature of reactivity.

In qualitative research one often hears the expression *'field research'* or 'fieldwork' used to indicate that data has been collected in a particular social context. However, some qualitative research is not really field research. For example, in oral history research, the data collected is largely based on interviews which may be conducted in any convenient location which is amenable to the respondent. The researcher relies upon the memory of the respondent to provide personalized accounts of the past experiences of the person. As the experiences are in the past, it is by definition not possible to re-live the exact experiences in their true social context. Edmondson and McManus (2007: 1156) provide an explanation of linking theory and methodology in fieldwork.

In ethnographic or participant observation research, on the other hand, the data is collected in a real-life social setting, such as in an urban environment, among a group of indigenous people, or among a closed religious community.

The significant aspect of field research is that the 'field' or social context has an important bearing upon the nature of the data. For example, in a closed religious community, the very 'closed' nature of the community has an inevitable effect upon the social interactions of the members. These interactions will often be restricted to the formalized and structured exchanges within the community. There will also almost certainly be an impact by the members of the community on the type of research questions asked and the responses given.

It is also important in this type of research to provide a detailed account of the nature of the field, so that the consumer of the research can appreciate how the nature of the data may have been changed by the social environment. It is often useful to describe these influences in a reflexive account.

Condensing and analysing data

One of the great pleasures of collecting and reading qualitative data is its very richness, and the way in which it enables respondents to discuss some of their most profound feelings about complex issues. Once respondents begin to feel comfortable and relaxed, they often talk a great deal. This conversational data is initially recorded electronically and then converted into a transcript, much like a script for a play. The transcription is often done by the researcher alone, but may also be carried out by a small team of researchers. In this case, different researchers are able to check their procedures with each other. When the transcription has been completed, it is also possible that it can be read by the respondents to enable them to verify and comment upon the content. The transcript carries the names of the different speakers (either actual, or more usually fictional) alongside their own dialogue. A relatively short period of conversation will normally convert into a very substantial amount of transcribed textual data. This quantity of data is both an advantage, but also potentially an inconvenience. The advantage lies in the very richness and detail of the data, but at the same time the researcher has the difficulty of converting this into a more easily understandable form.

The ultimate purpose of qualitative data and qualitative research is to distil the material into a form which constitutes a provisional theory. This theory has

the function, first, of condensing and simplifying the data, and also of expressing it in a more easily digestible form for future readers of the research.

The analysis of qualitative data involves a staged process of first of all identifying words, ideas and concepts which occur frequently throughout the text.
A word which occurs commonly throughout the text may be adopted as the
name of this group of ideas or concepts. The advantage of this strategy is that
it provides a sense of the distribution, and therefore perhaps of the importance,
of this idea throughout the text.

Let us imagine that you are conducting research into the various work roles
in a university. You gather data on a wide range of academic and administrative
roles throughout the institution. Let us suppose that you come across the term
'lecturer' very frequently in the data. This is a work role which is largely a
teaching role, although it will probably include the requirement to conduct a
minimal amount of research and to report this research in the form of journal
articles or conference publications. The term 'lecturer' would be known as a
'*code*', and the process of identifying this code would be termed 'coding'. Having identified the code of lecturer you could now annotate your transcripts
manually, or open files on a computer program for qualitative analysis.

The next stage in the analysis would be to identify a broader grouping which
includes several codes. For example, we might think of a group which includes
both lecturers, professors and full-time researchers. We might decide to term
this group 'academics'. We would describe this broader group as a '*category*'.
Members of this category are involved in both teaching and research, although
in different proportions. The lecturer normally does more teaching than
research, while the professor and the researcher normally place an emphasis
on research, with a smaller amount of teaching.

A further stage in the analysis would be to develop more general groupings
still, known as '*themes*'. There are roles in universities which involve teaching,
research and management. Some lecturers, for example, have to manage a particular academic course and those who teach on it. Some professors have to
manage research teams or units. Some professors might also be Deans of Faculty, and combine research, teaching and the management of a large subject
area. Staff involved in teaching, research and management might be known as
'managers'.

The development of codes, categories and themes would provide a framework to enable you to analyse your data, and to ultimately develop a provisional theory of work roles in a university. You would attempt, for example, to
hypothesize connections or correlations between some of the groupings, or
perhaps even to suggest provisional causal connections.

Approaches to preparing and presenting results

When analysing qualitative data, and presenting your results, there are a number of important factors to bear in mind. Significant among these is that you

should be transparent about the manner in which you have gone about analysing the data. For example, if several different researchers were provided with the same body of data, each person might identify different codes, categories and themes. They may not apply the same process of reasoning to the analysis, and certainly might devise different names for the different analytic groups. Hence, in order for other researchers to understand the analytic process, and build upon that if necessary, they need to be able to understand the researcher's thought process.

As part of this explanatory process, it is also important to present examples of quotations from the data, to illustrate the way in which codes and other groupings were developed. An important element of the data presentation process is to condense the data in order to make it more manageable to read. It is therefore useful if the data quotations are not too long, and yet provide sufficient information to justify the development of codes and categories.

A key purpose of this process of identifying codes, categories and themes is to search for potential connections between different facets of the data. For example, in the theme of 'managers' mentioned above, we may want to explore the relationship between a lecturer who manages a course team for a Master's programme, and a Dean of Faculty who manages a number of Bachelor's and Master's degrees within the same subject area. The lecturer may be responsible for the day-to-day organization of their course, while the Dean may focus upon the overall success and quality of a number of such degrees. In effect, once the different groupings have been identified, the next important stage is to explore the ways in which these groupings relate to each other.

The hypothetical relationships between codes and categories may be shown in a variety of ways in your article or thesis. This is one of the creative aspects of qualitative research, in that you can use your initiative to display the codes and categories in interesting and novel ways. These may involve a range of graphical techniques, such as flow charts, which can make it easier for readers to absorb the ideas of the relationships you are suggesting. Ultimately you will probably wish to express your developing theory in written form, but the graphical techniques may enhance the understanding process for the reader.

As your theory develops, you will wish to test it in a range of different social settings, in order to explore whether the theory is, in principle, generalizable. You may find that elements of your theory can be transferred to other contexts, while other parts of it seem only applicable to the original situation in which the data was collected. This is part of the gradual process of refining your theory, until it reaches a stage of maximal relevance to a range of social situations. Having examined in general terms, ways of presenting the data in a research study, we will now move on to discuss in detail the different methods and theoretical orientations associated with the collection of data.

Learning content

In this chapter you should have become familiar with the following ideas:

- category
- causal connection
- code
- constructionism
- correlation
- falsification
- field research
- reactivity
- reflexive or reflective account
- research aims
- social constructionism
- theme
- theoretical framework
- theoretical paradigm
- theoretical perspective
- transcription
- variable

Chapter 7

Phenomenological research

Chapter summary

This chapter examines the nature of phenomenology as the basis for research studies, and in particular the study of the way in which social actors create meaning from everyday events. The chapter emphasizes the way in which researchers should try to ignore their assumptions about the functioning of everyday life, and attempt to understand the perspectives of the social actors involved in the research context.

Subjectivity

Phenomenology gains its name from being the study of 'phenomena' or we could say the study of experiences which we come across in our lives. It is a particular feature of the phenomenological approach that we, as researchers, give priority to the views, experiences, perceptions and impressions of the research participants rather than those of the researchers. It is not that we do not value our own ability to describe and analyse the social world, but simply that we give pre-eminence to the viewpoints of the people who actually live the social life which we are investigating. Phenomenology was established as a distinct school of philosophy by the German philosopher, Edmund Husserl (1859–1938). It was later adapted as a research technique in the social sciences by the Austrian sociologist, Alfred Schütz (1899–1959). Phenomenology has much in common with a number of other qualitative approaches, including symbolic interactionism. For further discussion of the history of phenomenology, see Sokolowski (2000: 211).

Advice for students 7.1

Perhaps because phenomenology started as a philosophical concept, the terminology which is used can sometimes seem rather complex. Indeed, it can tend to obscure the ideas inherent in the approach. In fact, as I hope this chapter will demonstrate, the basic concepts of phenomenology are not particularly complicated. My advice would be that when studying phenomenology and reading around the subject, select texts which seem straightforward to you, and do not make the subject any more complex than it need be.

The phenomenological perspective is one which is predominantly concerned with the views of who we might term the *social actors* involved in a particular social situation. The social actors are those individuals who make the situation what it is. In a theatrical production the actors interpret the roles from the drama script to create a particular view of the world. In a similar way the social actors in a situation interact with each other to construct a particular vision of the world. Phenomenological researchers are primarily interested in both this interactive process and also in the actors' views of the social phenomena which are part of the social setting being studied.

In fact, phenomenologists do not consider a particular social setting as 'real' in the sense of being a fixed construction, but rather as an entity which is being continually adapted by the actors who take part in it. As an example, we could take the changing perceptions of the world of work. During the period of western industrialization in the late nineteenth and early twentieth centuries, there was an assumption that the workplace was largely male-dominated, often because the majority of work roles involved heavy, arduous labour. Workers lived in close proximity to factories, and worked long hours. However, with the advent of the technological revolutions of the late twentieth century, service roles began to replace many of the roles which existed in heavy manufacturing. More recently still, with the focus on information technology, it was no longer necessary to have a fixed locus of work. People could be increasingly flexible in choosing a workplace. We have, therefore, moved from a single, fixed concept of work to a situation of multiple roles, where people can work on their computers in many different locations.

The phenomenological researcher is likely to be interested in how the employees of today view the world of work. The workers of today have never experienced life in a Victorian mill, and thus can scarcely be expected to make a comparison with contemporary practices. Nevertheless, the contemporary worker may experience a series of work-related problems when sitting with a computer in a coffee bar. How does the remote worker cope when the computer system does not function properly? Are there issues of computer security when working in a public location? How does the remote worker gain access to management support, or help with problematic decision-making?

Phenomenologists, then, apply their own consciousness to the elaboration of *social meaning* in the world which surrounds them. For many, indeed most people, work or employment is primarily concerned with earning money. People work principally to earn sufficient money to feed themselves, to pay for somewhere to live, and to care for their families. In other words, people generally work for very pragmatic and utilitarian purposes concerned with physical survival in the world. However, many people attribute other categories of meaning to employment. For some, employment is also a means of staving off isolation in the world, and engaging in social intercourse and conversation. Work may also provide opportunities for generating a sense of self-fulfilment in the world; for finding feelings of purpose and creativity in a world which may otherwise appear rather isolating and alienating. This is close to what the humanistic psychologist, Abraham Maslow (1908–1970) termed 'self-actualization'.

Work may also provide opportunities for self-promotion, and for increasing one's social status. Different people may place different degrees of emphasis upon these aspects of work, but it does seem evident that most people do apply their consciousness to creating a sense of meaning in relation to the world. This process of seeking to create meaning in the world is sometimes known as intentionality. The meanings which are created by social actors are essentially subjective. Each social actor applies a range of influences including environmental and genetic factors, in order to create a subjective understanding of the social world in which they find themselves. The subjectivity of participants in phenomenological research is discussed by Koopman (2015: 3).

The interpretations of social actors

In the positivist tradition of research, it is normal for the researcher to be perceived as separate from the research process involving the participants or respondents. To put this another way, the researcher is not seen as contributing to, or as a significant part of, the research setting. The researcher manages the sampling, the data collection process and the data analysis, but is not assumed to have any effect upon the research context.

In the phenomenological, qualitative tradition, however, the researcher is perceived as occupying a central role in the research. There is an assumption that the researcher affects the research setting through factors such as the selection of topics for the interview questions, and the manner in which questions are asked.

Advice for students 7.2

When conducting phenomenological research, it is a good idea to reflect upon ways in which you as the researcher have an effect upon the research environment. There are many ways in which this might take place. Much depends, for example, upon the way in which you set up the research environment. This might be in a workplace, or perhaps in a domestic situation. Different environments might have an effect upon the way respondents answer questions. Another way in which you could affect the research environment is through the way in which you ask questions. Generally, the more supportive your manner, the more respondents will be inclined to talk and reveal their feelings about an issue. When you are actually writing your thesis, it would be a good idea to include a short section on the ways in which you tried to create the most positive research environment, and as far as you can tell, the consequences this had for the data collection process.

Imagine, for example, a research study of the nature of social care for the elderly in society. The researchers may be considerably younger than the respondents in the research study, and yet they know that they too will gradually get older, and will need the very type of care which they are researching. The researchers too are part of the society which needs to support, in one way or another, the care of the elderly. Relatives of the researchers may themselves be in need of care. All of these factors anchor the researchers in the project, and make them an essential component of the research.

Although the researchers may sketch out the kind of social, economic and ethical issues which they wish to explore, there are likely to be a number of situations throughout the data collection where they can direct and redirect the discussions. Thus, for example, if the participants are discussing the funding of adult social care through their own privately-held resources, the researchers may redirect discussion through a mention of funding via the public purse. This may or may not reflect the personal views of the researchers.

Setting aside everyday assumptions

One of the central aspects of the phenomenological perspective is that the researchers try to set on one side their own personal views, beliefs and assumptions concerning the issue being investigated. Phenomenologists often speak of 'bracketing' assumptions on one side. This concept is discussed further in Chan et al. (2013: 2). The reason for this approach is that human beings tend to acquire a wide variety of beliefs which become so much a part of our thinking, that we take them for granted. We do not tend to challenge them, but take them for granted, as if they are irrevocably true. This may be useful in some ways, in everyday life, but if we are trying to make sense of society, it may indeed be a handicap. It can tend to block or distort our understanding of society. During our lives, these belief systems or world-views can become very firmly embedded in our consciousness, and it is no easy job to divest ourselves of them, in order that we can see data and the social world around us, in a transparent, clear and unfettered way.

Most people subscribe to some sort of world-view, or at least they attach themselves to a particular vision of the world which is both life-enhancing and helps them to make sense of the world. Religious and political beliefs provide the most obvious forms of world-view, but popular music, films, theatre and sports can provide a range of different beliefs and ideologies.

Many of these belief systems contain implicit or explicit values and ways of behaving. When playing sports, for example, not only are there specific rules governing the sport, but there are often unwritten implicit codes of behaviour which govern general social interaction while the game is being played. Such codes of behaviour establish norms for determining what kind of actions are deemed to be polite, courteous and generally conducive to a pleasant experience within the particular sport. Now norms of behaviour generally have a positive influence because they help the playing of a sport to progress in an amenable way. However, if they gradually become a taken-for-granted set of regulations, which become rather rigid in their application, then they may have a more negative influence.

Phenomenology tends to challenge norms and values which have become rather entrenched. As a research method, phenomenology tries to explore with the respondents what they really feel and think about the phenomena under study, examining in as much detail as possible the deeper meanings and beliefs. In this sense, phenomenology is more concerned with an accurate description of people's feelings, motivation and thought processes, rather than trying to explain the way cognitive processes work.

Case study 7.1

Imagine that you wanted to research the situation of people changing jobs. You were interested in their emotions, how they feel both on leaving their previous workplace, and on starting their new job. This can be a major transition in people's lives, and you are interested in the stresses created and the ways in which people cope with moving into a new work environment. This research question would be suitable to investigate using a phenomenological perspective since work transition is an experience which raises deep feelings in many people, and a phenomenological approach would encourage respondents to reveal some of these.

The term 'transcendental phenomenology' is sometimes employed where the purpose of the research is to encourage respondents to describe the essential elements of the topic under study. However, it is not always easy for respondents to achieve this. Transcendental phenomenology is discussed further in Moerer-Urdahl and Creswell (2004: 20). Let us suppose that we ask a small group of respondents to discuss their experience of having an allotment. Some may focus upon the social element; some may regard it as a means of maintaining personal fitness in the open air; some may want to grow vegetables to donate to charity; while others may see it as part of their commitment to a vegetarian or vegan philosophy of life. Almost certainly a range of different ideals and philosophies will emerge from interviews with allotment holders, which may well be at odds with the traditional conception of the allotment. Indeed, one of the main consequences of phenomenology is that it enables respondents and researchers to offer contrary world-views to those traditionally associated with a particular phenomenon. It poses alternatives to the received wisdom of a research topic.

The ultimate purpose of transcendental phenomenology is to try to focus upon the central meaning of the research question for an individual respondent. As the research process is repeated for other respondents, there may be similarities for different people as they reveal commitments to similar basic experiences. There may also be the potential for extrapolation to other contexts. For example, in the case of a vegan philosophy in the allotment movement, this may be related to other world-views such as purchasing vegetable-based products, and not wearing shoes and other products which are made of leather.

A number of terms are used to refer to the concept of trying to eliminate the assumptions which we make about the everyday world. These terms include the Greek-derived *epoché*, bracketing, suspension of judgement and *phenomenological reduction*. They all share the notion of trying to remove accumulated bias, and to see the world in its original nature, without the subsequent accretions brought about through culture or social interactions. A related term is *eidetic reduction*, which seeks to emphasize the search for the essential elements of a phenomenon as opposed to the gradual accumulations of everyday life. According to the tenets of phenomenology, it is human consciousness which leads us towards the essence of reality, rather than the consequences of social interaction.

Exploring situations in depth

The nature of sampling in phenomenological research is very different from that in quantitative methods. It would not be at all unusual to have a sample size of one, or a slightly larger sample of up to 20 respondents. The basic issue is that since phenomenology is concerned with collecting data, which is as detailed as possible, the actual numerical size of the sample is less crucial. The actual sample size can be determined by the apparent requirements of the research and the possibility of identifying respondents who are willing to engage in detailed discussion and exploration of an issue.

Case study 7.2

Suppose that you decide to research the academic atmosphere, lifestyle of students, and the career destination of students in an art college. You are aware of your own preconceptions of art students existing within a very liberal, creative and relaxed lifestyle. You want to set these assumptions aside, and to explore the reality of art school courses, and the approach of students to the problem of earning a living after graduation. This research question would probably lend itself to a phenomenological approach, given the intention of trying to bracket off previous assumptions. The research could also probably be conducted with a small sample of fewer than ten respondents, making sure that they were selected on the basis of their willingness to articulate a detailed picture of art school life.

Of course, phenomenological research does make considerable demands upon the respondents. By its very nature, phenomenology is asking respondents to openly discuss issues which are often rather personal and intimate. At the same time researchers are placing themselves in the position of encouraging respondents to do this. Quite apart from ethical issues involved in this process, it can be very difficult for respondents to discuss very personal issues. Although we may know internally how we feel about something, trying to express that in words can be very different. If someone asks us how we feel about being a parent, we may have some ideas about our response to this, but expressing these ideas in an articulate fashion may not be easy. Equally, because of the personal nature of some issues, participants may be selective in terms of the material they choose to reveal.

For this reason, accounts of phenomenological research often try to ensure the anonymity of respondents, typically by employing fictional names in transcripts. In addition, researchers may give the transcripts of interviews to respondents to enable them to verify their accuracy.

In phenomenology, we can begin to see some of the distinct advantages of qualitative methods in contrast to quantitative approaches. It is very difficult in the positivist tradition to gain an appreciation of meaning and experience within human consciousness. Positivist techniques have a tendency to be too superficial to accumulate data which is deeply insightful and profound. However, on the other hand, it has to be said that data gathered from a phenomenological approach is rather difficult to apply to other contexts. There are possibilities to generalize from phenomenological data to other contexts, particularly if data is available from multiple sources, and can be triangulated.

Description and explanation

It is probably sufficiently complex for respondents to describe an aspect of their lives, without at the same time trying to explain how the situation has come about. In the case of being a parent, for example, we may be able to describe a situation where we have a serious difference of opinion with one of our children, but trying to explain the nuances of how this argument came about is a very different issue. For example, one of the typical sources of conflict between parents and teenagers is that parents usually want their children to become established in a conventional career. Children, on the other hand, want to take a gap year, go hitch-hiking and travelling, or take up an unusual occupation which does not have any particular career prospects. There must be innumerable parents and their offspring who discuss these issues interminably. A phenomenologist would be interested in discussing with parents or children the way in which they look at this issue. On the other hand, it may be difficult to explore the reasons for their holding the views which they do, as there is no intention within phenomenology to test hypotheses.

Phenomenologists seek to describe the world from the perspective of the people living their lives within it. In the example above, they would want to produce an accurate description of the way parents tend to react when their teenage children inform them that they intend to spend the next nine months trekking around some distant part of the planet. Equally, they would want to describe the kind of justification used by teenagers when they argue for spending time travelling before they commit to a particular career.

It is also interesting that so many parents and children are confronted by these issues. Phenomenologists are interested in the way it comes to pass that these kinds of issues are so widespread within families, and produce the same kind of conflictual situations. It seems as if many of the same kind of attitudes, values, aspirations and hopes of young people and of their parents are widely distributed, irrespective almost of culture and society. Phenomenologists are interested in exploring these shared meanings and interpretations.

Individual perspectives on social situations

The main purpose of phenomenological research is to try to reveal the way individuals perceive society, by encouraging them to generate detailed accounts of the world around them. Sometimes these accounts are of interest in themselves, since they generate unanticipated interpretations of what phenomenologists sometimes refer to as the *life-world*, or their experience of the world as they live it. On other occasions, it is interesting to note the apparent similarities between the different accounts of people, and the way in which there tends to develop shared understandings of the social world. It seems as if, during the process of inter-subjective communication, people can develop shared understandings of the world which act as a means of *social cohesion*. The notion of the life-world is discussed in Honer and Hitzler (2015: 545).

Phenomenology emphasizes the way in which research respondents describe their lives and the particular significant moments in it. Some events or periods will almost certainly be more important for the respondent than others, and consequently the meaning for respondents will be more significant. We might consider the case of students receiving criticism from tutors for their college work, or of students receiving praise for their work. The researcher would ask respondents to describe their feelings in these circumstances, and perhaps compare the feelings of one student with those of another. This is one of the positive results of phenomenological research. It enables the researcher to examine the responses of people to similar situations, and therefore to enable respondents to perhaps adjust their behaviour and make it more relevant to situations as they occur.

One of the great strengths and values of phenomenology is that it enables us to gain an understanding of a life event, even though we may not have actually experienced that event ourselves. The life event may be, for example, a serious accident, an illness requiring major clinical intervention, or the death of a close relative. It is true that our understanding relies upon an account spoken by someone else, but nevertheless if the research is done thoroughly, then it provides us with an idea of the significance of the event for the respondent concerned. Phenomenological research enables us to begin to appreciate how others view the world around them, and how they find a sense of meaning in that world. This is not only of purely intellectual interest, but it provides us with a basis for helping fellow human beings in similar situations in the future.

There is also an aspect to phenomenology which is potentially radical, and can help us alter the way we, as a society, can respond to situations. Once we have a better understanding of the life experiences of our fellow human beings, we can adjust our responses to their situation. Society can be more effective in the help it provides for people, and may not simply continue with the accepted policies and strategies. The decision-makers of society can adjust their responses to difficult situations, and hopefully provide improved responses.

Learning content

In this chapter you should have become familiar with the following ideas:

- bracketing
- eidetic reduction
- *epoché*
- life-world
- phenomenological reduction
- phenomenology
- social actor
- social cohesion
- social meaning
- transcendental phenomenology

Chapter 8

Interview research

Chapter summary

The use of interviews is probably the commonest method employed in qualitative research. However, interview's apparent simplicity and straightforwardness belie the subtleties of its use. This chapter explores the many nuances of the use of interviews. It examines the different ways in which interviews can be structured, and the variety of methods for designing questions. The issue of the validity of interview data is discussed, along with the question of potential bias in the interviewer. The chapter also discusses the practical arrangements of the interview, particularly so that the interviewee can feel relaxed, and able to provide valid and reliable data.

Organization of the interview: including single and group interviews

The organization of an interview may appear to be deceptively simple. It may seem to be just a matter of sitting down with someone and asking a few questions. In fact, in order to collect valid research data in a manner which is acceptable to respondents requires a good deal of careful planning. There are also a good many ethical issues which arise in interview research.

Once you have selected the subject of your research, and decided that in principle you would like to employ the interview method, then you will need to turn your attention to the question of selecting respondents or interviewees. From the very start, it is worth giving as much thought as possible to the research from the interviewee's point of view. When you first approach potential interviewees, there will probably be many questions which will occur to them.

First of all, they will probably want to understand the nature of the research, and feel confident that they are able to answer any questions put to them. You will therefore have to give some thought to explaining your research in a clear and straightforward manner. They will also want information on practical matters, such as the location and time of the interview, and whether it will fit in with their other commitments. As the interviewees start to think more about the implications of taking part, they may start to ask themselves more complex questions. Will the interview include any personal questions? If I don't want to answer a question, will that be acceptable? If I start to feel nervous, can I end the interview? Will my answers to questions be recorded or written down? If so, will they be passed on to other people? Will my identity be kept anonymous? These are all valid matters of concern to potential interviewees, and we will take up these issues as the chapter progresses. Further discussion of the issue of identifying interviewees can be found in Seidman (2019: 45).

Interviewees may also want to know whether they will be interviewed on their own, or as part of a group. This is an issue which you will probably consider as part of your research design. A series of one-to-one interviews is very useful for comparing the responses of different interviewees with regard to the same research question. Sometimes, however, it is useful to conduct interviews with a small group of respondents, called a *focus group*. In this way discussions can take place simultaneously between respondents, and the interactions can be very useful in terms of illuminating research issues.

Let us now consider some of the potential interviewee concerns mentioned above. Depending upon the research topic, it is possible that an interview may include some personal themes. For example, in a research study of the standards of care in a hospital, respondents may be asked about their own experiences of health care. Nevertheless, respondents should be reassured that there is no compulsion to answer any questions which they feel are too personal. If respondents feel that they do not want to answer a question, then they should be encouraged to say so, and this wish will be respected. Indeed, respondents may begin to feel that the entire interview is becoming too intrusive. If that is the case, then they should be aware that they have an absolute right to end the interview. Respondents may have a lot of concerns about the recording of the interview, whether this is done electronically or simply by taking notes. They may have concerns that their views will be recorded for posterity, and could be passed on to others at any time in the future. It should be explained to them that the sole purpose of keeping a record of interviews is to provide accurate research data. Once the research has been completed, then the recording or notes will be destroyed. However, it should be explained to respondents that the account of the research, whether that be a thesis or a journal article, will contain quotations and extracts from the interview. The reason for this is to justify arguments, and generally to provide evidence for the conclusions drawn from the research.

Clearly, a range of people will have access to the data extracts in a thesis or article, but the important issue is really that every attempt will be made to ensure the anonymity of the interviewees. This can be done by allocating fictional names to the data extracts, or simply not using any names.

A practical issue here is that all of these reassurances may have to be given to each interviewee prior to each interview. This can be very laborious and it may be that the advice given is sometimes not totally consistent. This is where it can be useful to prepare a written summary of both the nature of the research and of the organizational proceedings for the interview. This can then be given to all potential interviewees with the aim of trying to ensure that they all receive the same information. In terms of the research, it will probably be a good idea to explain why you are approaching the potential respondents. For example, they may have something in their background which is relevant to the research, or they may have previously expressed an interest in the research. Interviewees will probably want to know how the research will help people. This may well enhance their motivation to provide data for the research.

In terms of the organization of the interviews, respondents will need information on practical matters such as the names of contact persons managing the research; phone numbers, postal and email addresses; and maps of the institution in which the interviews will take place. They will also need to know the planned dates and time slots for proposed interviews. Some interview research provides the opportunity for interviewees to read the transcripts, and to correct them if they feel that they are not a faithful record of what they said. If this is to take place, then the procedures should be outlined and agreed by those concerned. Further discussion of the transcription of interview data is available in McLellan et al. (2003: 65).

The setting of the interview

A research interview is a sensitive and sophisticated interaction between two people, in the case of a one-to-one interview. In the case of a group interview or focus group, the interactions become no less complex, simply because there are a number of people involved (see Nyumba et al., 2018: 21, for further discussion of focus groups). The apparently smallest of factors can sometimes have a major effect upon the interview, and perhaps distort the nature of the data provided. Many research interviews in the social sciences take place on university premises, and the formality of such settings may have an effect upon the way the interviewee perceives the social setting. It should be added briefly here that ethnographic or field interviews often take place in the actual social setting for the research, and there are some special considerations to be borne in mind here. More will be said about ethnographic interviews in Chapter 9.

It is important to bear in mind that when interviews are conducted in a formal setting, every effort should be made to create a relaxing environment for the interviewee. A room should be reserved, ideally with a glass panel in the door in order not to create a 'closed' atmosphere. If the interview is being recorded, then the recording system should be explained to the interviewee. It should also be explained that the interviewee can turn off the recorder if at any time they feel they do not want their comments to be recorded. This provides the respondent with a feeling of control over the proceedings. Before the real interview commences, it may be a good idea for the researcher and interviewee to have an informal discussion, in order to help them both feel relaxed. A research interview is not something which should be rushed. One of the strengths of the process is that the respondents should feel able to take their time, and reflect carefully upon the issues raised.

It is worth remembering that research interviews can often give the impression of a power differential between the interviewer and the interviewee. The interviewer may represent a sense of authority and knowledge to the interviewee, which may intimidate the latter to some extent. Interviewers may be advised to wear informal, casual dress, for example, and to adopt any strategy in the layout of the interview room which makes the respondent feel at ease. From the beginning of the interview the interviewer should try to create an atmosphere of listening, rather than continually asking penetrating questions. As a researcher it is worth always remembering that it is the opinions, feelings and impressions of the interviewee in which you are interested that are important.

It is probably in a traditional one-to-one interview that you can best understand the perspectives of the respondent, but there are other ways in which research interviews can be arranged. Focus groups in which a number of respondents are asked to discuss an issue, perhaps prompted by a researcher, can be a useful means of initiating discussion. The interaction between respondents can encourage members of the group to formulate ideas on an issue.

Interviews can also be arranged so that they take place *remotely*. The interview can take place by telephone, or by a visual connection on the internet. These methods have a number of logistical advantages, notably in terms of avoiding travelling time. The respondent can also be interviewed in their own familiar setting, which may make them feel rather more confident in terms of the process. It may be argued, on the other hand, that something is lost in these arrangements, in terms of the closeness of the interaction between interviewer and interviewee. A further variant in the interview process is that it takes place in real time through email. Questions are put to the respondent by email and the latter then types a reply. This process may be rather slow and artificial, but it may be deemed an advantage that the exchanges exist in written form from the beginning, and no transcription is needed. Whatever structural methods are arranged for the interview, the interviewer should try as far as possible to be accepting of the viewpoints of the respondent, even if they do not concur with their own perspective. If the interviewer gives any impression of rejecting the views of the respondent, then this can have an adverse effect upon the willingness of the respondent to continue to offer their views. The interviewer should truly adopt the role of a facilitator, gently encouraging the respondent to provide their viewpoints on an issue. It is also helpful if the environment chosen for the interview is not one which is liable to interruptions or disturbances, and is relatively private.

Interviewees are generally very interested in what initiated the research project in which they might come to be involved. This is particularly so if the research has a philanthropic element, and should in principle bring about a clear improvement in the quality of human life. If the research project is clearly designed to help other people, then this can be very motivating for the interviewees.

One final consideration for the interview is the way in which the interview should be started, and the way in which it should be concluded. The manner in which these two functions are achieved is important in terms of encouraging the respondent to feel positive about the research.

Advice for students 8.1

The following is an example of how as a researcher you might go about introducing the interview process:

Hello. My name is ... and I am a lecturer here in this department. I would like to say how much we appreciate your coming this morning, and helping us with our research. We are trying to improve our facilities and approaches to teaching mature students in higher education. All of the people being interviewed this morning are either retired or approaching retirement in a few years, and are interested in doing a higher education course as part of their retirement activities. As I said in my letter, we would like to record the interview, but I must stress that you do not have to respond to a question if you feel it is too intrusive. The questions I am going to ask are really very straightforward and designed to enable you to talk about your feelings about higher education, and why you would like to pursue education at this stage in your life. May I stress that if at any stage in the interview, you would like to take a rest, then just switch off the recorder using this button here.

Is that all right? Do you have any questions before we start?

The more supportive and encouraging the introduction, then the more likely that the respondents will provide useful, detailed data, and that the research project as a whole will be a success. It is also very important though that the interview is ended on a positive note, and that the interviewee leaves the room feeling that they have enjoyed the process, and that what they have said will be useful for the project.

Advice for students 8.2

The following is an example of how you might go about concluding the interview, and leaving the interviewee with a positive feeling about the research.

Well, thank you very much for taking part in this interview. I hope you have enjoyed it and perhaps found it useful. You certainly gave me some very interesting replies, and this should help our research project a lot.

Let me just reassure you that your real name will not be used in any research report, although we will use extracts from what you have said.

There should not be any way in which what you have said can be traced back to you. So, we hope this research will encourage more mature students to study at the university. If you would like to receive a copy of the final research report, I would be delighted to send you a copy.

Finally, if you have any questions about the research, I would be very happy to try to answer them.

Structured, semi-structured and unstructured interviews

Interviews are often categorized as being one of three types: *structured, semi-structured* or *unstructured*. This is a convenient convention and I will adhere to it in this chapter, although it is probably more accurate to think of interview types as existing in a range from very formal and structured to extremely informal and unstructured, with a wide number of variations in between.

It is worth also considering that there are important philosophical features of each of the types of interview. The structured interview tends to rest upon the assumption that the interviewer is able to define the key issues of the research topic, and to frame appropriate questions for the interviewee. It is further assumed that these questions will tend to be *closed questions* which have a response capable of being articulated in a brief, clear manner.

At the other extreme are the unstructured interviews. These assume that neither the interviewer nor the interviewee has a comprehensive appreciation of the research issue, and that the interview process should involve more of a joint exploration and examination of the research questions. Questions will reflect this exploratory function and tend to be *open questions*, leaving the opportunity for genuine exploration and compromise.

Between these two extremes exist a wide range of variations, combining some of the features of structured and some of the features of unstructured interviews.

Whichever method is adopted, interviewers generally use notes of some kind to support them during the interview. These notes may include examples of questions to be asked or simply brief summaries of themes to be explored. These notes are generally known as an *interview schedule*. In the case of a structured interview the schedule is usually a formal document. It may start with a summary of the research, and of the interview process. It will often be followed by a list of the questions to be asked. Incorporated in this list may be a series of response boxes which the interviewer can use to code the responses from the respondent. There will probably finally be some assurances about anonymity and confidentiality, and an opportunity for the interviewee to ask any questions which have occurred to them during the interview.

It is an important feature of such interview schedules that the questions are asked in the same order and in the same way, to all respondents. It is equally important that the text about the research project should be read out in the same manner to all interviewees. If respondents do not understand a question, then they should not generally be permitted to seek clarification, as this would probably introduce an element of individuality and variation to the interview. There is a good deal of similarity between a questionnaire and an interview schedule which is highly structured. However, the schedule can be adapted and varying degrees of informal discussion introduced to create a semi-structured interview.

At the other extreme is the unstructured interview. For this type of interview the schedule may only consist of a brief series of research themes or topics, which act as prompts for the interviewer. The latter will generally adapt the order in which these are discussed, depending upon the course of the conversation. Equally, the way in which the interview develops may depend upon the interests and inclinations of the interviewee.

The unstructured interview is arguably the most closely related philosophically to the principles of qualitative, interpretive research. It tends to avoid the idea of external researchers who impose their concept of the world upon the data collection process. Rather, the unstructured interview encourages a feeling of equality between interviewer and interviewee. They both contribute ideas to the discussion, and work on combining their world-views in analysing the research question in hand.

Case study 8.1

If you are conducting research on an issue which is fundamentally ethical in nature, then the unstructured interview can be a very suitable means of collecting data. Such research issues might be the maintenance of discipline in schools, or the best strategies for rehabilitating prisoners. Giving the interviewee a lot of freedom to explore an issue such as these enables them to range far and wide in terms of analysing moral complexities. They may also raise issues which you as the researcher had not previously considered.

Advantages and disadvantages of interviews

The interview is an extremely popular method of collecting data, although, as with all research methods, there are some disadvantages. The following discussion relates primarily to semi-structured and unstructured interviews as these are the types most closely connected with qualitative approaches. Let us consider the advantages of interviews first of all.

Most of the people who have experienced the research interview process seem to have enjoyed it by and large. For the interviewee, there is the opportunity to express their opinions about an issue, and to articulate their viewpoints, while the interviewer can learn about the views of others. This exchange of views and opinions encourages the production of well-informed and well-considered data, which can be the basis for a sound research report.

The interview process is also very flexible. If either party to the interview is not certain about what the other person has said, then they can ask for clarification. If the terminology being used seems too obscure or complex, then it can be simplified. In short, there is a great deal of flexibility in the interview process, to help both interviewer and respondent to get the most out of the process.

The fact that interviewer and interviewee are both facing each other enables additional non-verbal data to be collected. This includes such aspects as facial expressions, mannerisms and body posture. All of these may provide indications of feelings and attitudes.

Although it can be time-consuming to identify a sample of potential interviewees, once people have agreed to take part, there is usually only a relatively small number of people who do not come for their interview appointment. There is also the opportunity to adapt the time of the interview to the convenience of respondents.

During the interview there are a number of opportunities for obtaining more precise data. If a response appears to be rather vague, then the interviewer can ask more penetrating questions in order to try to get to the heart of an issue. If the interviewer wants to check the veracity of a response, then the same question can be asked later during the interview in a slightly different way. Alternatively, if the interviewee is willing, a repeat interview can be held at a later date. Further discussion of the advantages of interview research can be seen in Alshenqeeti (2014: 40).

Despite the many advantages of interviewee research, there can also be some disadvantages. A fairly obvious disadvantage of interview research is that it can take up a lot of time. There may be travelling involved to reach a respondent's home or place of work; and in order to do justice to the actual interview, it should be conducted at a calm, relaxed pace. It is possible that *bias* can develop during the interviews, with the interviewers permitting their own feelings and views to be embedded in the questions. Equally, the interviewees may find that they inadvertently or even deliberately give responses which they believe may be acceptable to the interviewers. Finally, there is also a danger that discussing some issues may prove to be rather delicate or contentious for either the interviewer or interviewee, or both.

Designing questions to employ

During a research interview, one of the interviewer's main responsibilities is to guide the developing dialogue in order that the respondent provides as much interesting and informative data as possible. In order to achieve this, there are a number of general strategies which can be adopted, quite apart from the features of the actual conversation.

As a general rule, you should try to ask questions which encourage the respondent to talk a great deal. The converse of this is also true, that you should try to avoid questions which can be answered with a one-word answer. Thus, 'Did you enjoy the film last night?' encourages a 'yes' or 'no' response. On the other hand, the question 'Could you describe the main features of the plot in the film last night?' encourages a much more discursive answer.

Sometimes there are periods of silence during an interview. This is not necessarily a problem. If you pause in the flow of questions, this may give thinking time to the respondent who may then be able to resume the interview by providing further responses to a question. There are other useful ways of encouraging the respondent to maintain the conversation. If you keep eye contact with the interviewee, it gives the impression of being interested in what is being said. Also, it is helpful to assume an 'open', friendly expression as this encourages responses from the interviewee. It is also worth remembering that the whole purpose of the interpretive interview is to encourage the respondent to articulate the main features of their own world-view. Every question should try to reveal as much as possible of the perspective of the respondent on the key research issues. To this end, it is important that you try to avoid, as much as possible, introducing your own viewpoints into the conversation. The more you talk about yourself and your own opinions, the more these are likely to influence the way in which the respondent replies to questions.

Research interviewers often draw a distinction between 'closed' and 'open' questions. Closed questions tend to focus upon a restricted element of a research issue, and encourage the response to consist either of a single word or only several words. For example, 'Who wrote the best-selling psychology text book ...?', or 'What was her main research interest?' The problem with these sorts of questions is that they do not encourage the interviewee to adopt an expansive approach and to talk freely about their own viewpoints.

Open questions, on the other hand, encourage respondents to reflect more upon their own ideas and to speak in a more discursive manner. A more open question would be 'Why do you feel that this particular psychologist was awarded the prize?' Even if the respondent does not speak for very long, a question formulation such as this offers the opportunity to ask further probing questions.

It is sometimes tempting to ask questions which contain within them a suggestion for a response. An example of such a leading question would be 'Do you think that the first article she published had an effect on the award of the prize?' These questions should be avoided because they may tend to reflect the interviewer's perspective and not that of the respondent.

At the beginning of the interview, it is a sensible strategy not to begin immediately with questions on the technical aspects of the interview. It is perhaps wisest to ask one or two general questions, perhaps commenting on the weather, or on a television programme. This will help the respondent to feel relaxed and better able to comment on the main interview questions. Another related issue is to try to avoid complex technical vocabulary when asking questions. Wherever possible, try to adopt the language register normally used by the respondent. In this case there are less likely to be misunderstandings caused by language, vocabulary or sentence structure. In short, there is a lot to be said for asking questions clearly and simply and using straightforward language.

Validity and reliability of interview data

In all kinds of research, whether quantitative or qualitative, we want to have confidence in the data we are collecting, and also in the conclusions which we draw from that data. There are two basic measures which are used to hopefully reassure us about what we might loosely term the accuracy of our data. These two measures are termed validity and reliability.

Validity is a measure of the extent to which our data collection instrument actually does measure what we hope and believe it is measuring. For example, we might ask our respondent, 'Do you get a sense of fulfilment from your present job?' The interviewee may answer 'yes' to this question because they do actually get a sense of satisfaction and reward from their job. In that case we can say that the question and the data we obtain have a high level of validity.

On the other hand, the respondents may also answer 'yes', but for different reasons. They may wish to present a positive image of themselves, and may therefore give an untruthful answer. In this case the data would have low validity. Now you may say that it is going to be very difficult to know whether our data is or is not valid. However, there are some strategies we can employ which give us clues about the validity of our data. Later on in the interview, we could ask a different version of the above question. Instead of asking whether the respondent gets a sense of fulfilment, we could ask 'Apart from a salary, what do you feel you gain from your job?' If the respondent talks about fulfilment, or a similar concept, then we may feel that this has corroborated the first 'yes' response, and confirmed the validity of the initial data. Another strategy involves asking the same question, but using a very different method. For example, you could ask a version of the question, but this time include it in a questionnaire. Again, if you got a similar response, you might feel that there was some validity in the original data. This approach could be described as methodological triangulation. Further discussion of validity can be found in Kuzmanić (2009: 43).

Case study 8.2

Let us suppose that you want to research some aspects of the lifestyle of young people involved in the drug culture. First of all, it may be difficult, but not impossible, to contact potential respondents who are willing to be interviewed. Assuming that you can contact a potential sample, you would have to be aware that there would be possible problems with the validity of the data. As the respondents are possibly involved in illegal activity, they may be less than honest in their responses, in order to protect themselves. However, it is possible that you could adopt strategies to check the validity of their responses. As part of the interview, you could ask them why they had agreed to take part in the interviews. If they appeared to have a legitimate reason, then this might shed some light on the veracity of their other replies.

The other main measure of the accuracy of data is known as *reliability*. Let us suppose that you interview a person and get a certain response. If you were to repeat the interview with the same person and question, a few weeks later, you would hope to receive the same response. If you did, then you could say that your data had a high level of reliability. In a perfect world, data should be both valid and reliable. However, there may be perfectly good reasons why a person's response changes over a period of time. One fairly obvious reason is that people change their minds over an issue. We know, for example, that a few weeks before a political election, people may decide to vote for one candidate, but when it comes to the actual election may vote for someone else. Nevertheless, reliability is a useful measure of the extent to which we can trust an interview response.

Potential bias

The one-to-one interview is a very personal event, in which there is ample opportunity for either party to unduly influence the other. The interviewer, for example, may ask questions in such a way that the response of the interviewee is affected. Equally, the interviewee may be affected by the interview situation in such a way that their responses are affected, particularly, for example, in terms of giving a response which is acceptable to the interviewer. These kinds of effects can give rise to bias in the interview, and hence undermine both the validity and reliability of the data.

It is probably true of many research interviews that when analysing the data, the interviewers use their own judgement to decide which aspects of the total data should be included in the final data analysis. This almost inevitably introduces some degree of bias to the analysis. Action can, however, be taken to limit these effects by asking other researchers to assist with the data analysis. Another way in which bias can be introduced by interviewers is when they ask closed questions. Under these circumstances it is relatively easy for respondents to provide the response which they feel is wanted by the interviewer. On the other hand, if the interviewer asks open questions, inviting a long and discursive response, then it is much more difficult for the respondent to construct a response which they feel would be acceptable to the interviewer. Interviewees may sometimes seek the approval of the interviewer by responding in a way which they feel would be acceptable. With closed questions where the respondent only has to answer yes or no, then it may be easier to deceive the interviewer. On the other hand, with open questions where the respondents have to provide more detailed, considered responses, this becomes more difficult.

It can sometimes happen that the interviewer and interviewee possess parallel world-views, and they may to some extent reinforce each other's opinion, leading to a measure of bias in responses. It can also happen that interviewer and interviewee both harbour a wish to be liked by the other member of the interview process, and that this affects the way in which they act and respond during the interaction. This again can introduce a degree of bias.

In a perfect world of course, a research interview would be a balanced and rational exchange. However, the issues mentioned above show that an element of bias can easily creep into the process. In general, one of the best ways of limiting the effects of bias is to involve other people in the interview process, for example, as observers, or as assistants in the analytic process. When participants know this is happening, it can often have the effect of limiting bias effects.

Learning content

In this chapter you should have become familiar with the following ideas:

- bias
- closed question
- focus group
- interview schedule
- open question
- reliability of interviews
- remote interview
- semi-structured interview
- structured interview
- unstructured interview
- validity of interviews

Chapter 9

Ethnographic research

Chapter summary
This chapter examines the nature of ethnographic research, and its development from earlier anthropological studies. It explores the purpose of ethnography in terms of obtaining a deep understanding of the culture of a research setting, and in so doing retaining the perspective of the respondents rather than of the researcher. The chapter examines, in particular, the different ways in which data may be collected and recorded. It also considers the important ethical questions of gaining access to the field, in a way which preserves a sensitivity towards, and empathy for, the respondents. The chapter also explores the different strategies which may be used by the researchers to embed themselves in the research environment.

Ethnography and anthropology

Anthropology is the study of other societies with a particular focus on such aspects as culture, social systems, family life and religious beliefs. Early anthropologists in the nineteenth century were often concerned with the collection of artefacts as exemplars of culture and society. There was, however, a developing awareness that in order to truly understand a different society, one needed to spend a sustained period of time living in that society. This viewpoint was particularly illustrated by the anthropologists Bronislaw Malinowski (1884–1942) and Margaret Mead (1901–78) during their fieldwork in the southern Pacific.

Anthropologists gradually realized that in order to fully appreciate the nature of a society, one needed to immerse oneself completely in the daily life of the societal members and to try to appreciate the significance of their social customs. Ideally, it would also be necessary to learn sufficient of the language in order to be able to participate in rituals and ask sufficient questions in order to grasp the meaning of local culture and practices. It is also probably true to say that the starting point for much of early anthropology was an ethnocentric perspective. This tended to involve an assumption that Western European culture was markedly superior to that of other societies. Further discussions on *ethnocentrism* are available in Hammond and Axelrod (2006: 927). As anthropological studies continued, however, including particularly fieldwork investigations, researchers began to develop an awareness of the relevance of comparative studies. Anthropologists became aware that it could be useful to compare their own culture with those of distant societies, particularly in relation to such aspects as social habits, lifestyle, morality and ethics, family life and marriage. From the notion of comparative social studies came the relatively radical idea of *cultural relativism*. This raised the question of whether one could assume that the customs of one society were superior to those of another society, or merely perhaps more relevant to the social environment of the culture in which they originated. In short, as we move into the twentieth century, there was an evolving viewpoint that it could be beneficial to be open-minded about other cultures, with a view to considering their relevance to what had previously been considered as the dominant cultures of the world. Ethnographic accounts of other societies thus became a very useful and important source of data for reflecting on our own western society. An analysis of the development of *ethnography* can be found in Ladner (2016: 15).

The further development which gradually took place in the twentieth century was that the creation of ethnographies or ethnographic accounts as a research method could be applied not only to distant societies, but to minority cultures within our own society. Hence sociologists realized that it was informative to collect ethnographic data on, for example, a school, a prison, or other institutions. Not only did such ethnographic studies of institutions provide insights into our own society on a broader level, but it was also possible to construct ethnographic accounts of micro elements of our own culture, such as groups of teenagers, football supporters or factory workers. Such studies provided social scientists with useful insight into the way in which social groups interacted within our own society. Not only did such ethnographies reveal a lot about the way in which contemporary society functioned, but also helped social and political planners propose ideas for the development of society. Hence ethnography is not only a very flexible method of investigating different facets of society, but it is also useful for developing strategies for the improvement of society.

It is also worth noting that the period immediately following the Second World War was a time of quite considerable mass movement of peoples, and of the dislocation of social structures. In the case of Britain, the war had resulted in significant labour shortages, and attempts were made to rectify these through the recruitment of people from the countries of the Commonwealth. This was a period of major economic migration which brought about social change in Britain on a very large scale. Communities with a wide range of different cultures and religions began to establish themselves in Britain, notably from the Caribbean and the Indian sub-continent. There was considerable interest in conducting ethnographic research which helped people to understand the customs and religions of these migrant groups. In the long run, this work may have done much to enhance inter-ethnic relations in the United Kingdom, and to support a broader tolerance between different social groups.

Reasons for adopting an ethnographic approach

The term 'ethnography' is sometimes used to describe the account of a society, social group or culture which results from the process of ethnographic research. An ethnography is thus the descriptive and analytic account which is the ultimate product of this type of investigation. One of the main reasons for using an ethnographic approach is therefore where there appears to be a need for a *holistic* account which links together many of the features of life in the social group in question. Ethnographies are typified by a variety of features. They present a very detailed portrait of a social group and the people who live within its confines. They employ an extremely wide range of data, which is integrated into a cohesive account of the culture of the group being investigated. While the ethnography seeks to present in great detail the cultural life of the society, it also seeks to respect the privacy, integrity and traditional lifestyle of the group. This is an important ethical consideration which often entails adopting a cautious and delicate approach to the collection and interpretation of data. Ethnographers have to be continually aware that ethnographic research can have unintended consequences on the group being investigated, and that this impact may not always be totally beneficial.

Advice for students 9.1

When you are writing up your postgraduate thesis, there are certain conventions with which you will need to comply. You will receive advice on these from your supervisor, and you can also consult previous theses. These conventions tend to have arisen within the context of a positivist tradition. However, qualitative and ethnographic theses are in the process of developing new conventions. Ethnographic theses can sometimes appear to be much more like 'telling a research story' than a formal research report. You may like to consult former ethnographic theses, and to develop an appreciation of the variety of thesis structures available, before selecting a structure for yourself. It is probably wise to select a suitable thesis structure and then emulate this. At least then you will be able to argue that you have emulated the pattern of a previous, successful thesis.

One of the principal ways of mitigating the potential effects of intrusion into a social group is for the researcher to develop contacts with the group in a very gradual way. It is unreasonable to expect the members of a group will admit a stranger into their midst, and immediately start revealing intimate aspects of their lives to them. As researchers, we should expect an ethnographic study to take a long time, and for contact with the social members to take place gradually. As the members of the social group begin to embrace the presence of the researcher, they normally reveal more and more about their lifestyle, customs and values. This is to the advantage of the researcher, but also helps to build confidence in the social members.

One of the significant reasons for employing an ethnographic perspective is that the approach uses a wide range of different types of data. This data can include observations, field notes, audio and video recordings, artefacts and photographs. The data can also be collected by using different methods such as *participant observation* and interviews. Therefore, when conducting research, the ethnographer can often make use of the widest and sometimes most unusual of data to gradually construct a picture of the social context.

The viewpoint of the subject

One of the most important facets of ethnography is that it emphasizes the interpretation and world-view of the subjects of the study. The researcher is trying above all else to understand the world from the point of view of the social actor. In a study of football supporters, for example, the ethnographic approach would try to reveal and understand the significance of the chanting, of the sometimes violent behaviour, of the confrontational approach with opposition supporters, and of the sense of dedication felt by many supporters. The research would try to reveal what it feels like to actually be a football supporter, rather than to take for granted the assumptions of the researcher. For example, even though the popular image of football supporters is that they participate sometimes in confrontational behaviour, this may not be the perception of the actual supporters.

To take another fictional example, let us consider the nature of an ethnographic study of holiday makers in Spain. The study would not try to reveal the perceptions and impressions of the researchers, but rather try to understand the world-view of those people who choose a beach holiday in Spain. The researchers are trying to understand the reasons for people selecting Spain for a holiday; the aspects of their own culture which the holiday makers hope to find in Spain; and the aspects of Spanish culture which attract them. In short, one of the challenges of ethnography is for the researchers to learn to discard their own assumptions and prejudices, and to encourage the research subjects to articulate their own views on an issue.

Insider research and auto-ethnography

The aim of a great deal of ethnography is for the researcher to be accepted within the social group being researched. The aim is that the researcher becomes so much an element of the researched group that this gives a legitimacy to the data, and the respondents become very accepting of the researcher. This level of acceptance can be achieved in a variety of ways, notably by spending a great deal of time with the respondents and gradually gaining their confidence. It is often the case, however, that the researcher and respondents share some element of their lives, or have certain characteristics in common, such that the researcher is accepted within the social group being studied.

An example of this type of situation is the general category of work-based research. This is where someone works in an organization, and for various reasons decides to conduct some research on a situation within that organization. Many teachers who are pursuing higher degrees decide to conduct research within the school, college or university in which they teach. They may study a variety of themes including, for example, social relations in the staffroom, staff hierarchies and management, the role of the headteacher, teaching styles, curriculum issues and the ethics of teaching situations. These are just a few examples of the kinds of themes which can be addressed by a *teacher-researcher*. By being an insider, a *de facto* member of the group being investigated, the teacher-researcher can understand many of the subtleties of the social interactions taking place. This gives teacher-researchers a methodological advantage when compared with external researchers who have little idea of how the relationships function in a school community. Teacher-researchers often know how to collect data in unusual settings, and how to locate key informants. On the other hand, it can often be difficult for colleagues of the researcher to appreciate that they have two different roles. On the one hand, they are a normal member of staff, but, on the other, they have this separate role which involves observing their colleagues and pupils, and writing about them. This can sometimes lead to tensions. For example, during discussions in the staffroom, colleagues may wonder whether the researcher is adopting the role of data gatherer, or is simply being a normal colleague.

A related problem is that the insider researcher in a situation is already familiar with many of the features and circumstances which are particular to that social context. They may be familiar with the idiosyncrasies of a specific pupil or teacher, or they may take for granted the particular ways of organization and functioning which are typical of that school. Because they take so much for granted, they may not be able to objectively view the characteristics of the school, and this may limit their role as a researcher. On the other hand, an outsider researcher, who moves into the research field, may view everything as 'strange' and therefore produce a more objective ethnographic account.

The insider knowledge of some teacher-researchers may mean that they predetermine the themes to be researched, and even the questions to be asked. This is in many ways antithetical to the process of ethnographic research which normally seeks to expose and examine the participants' view of the world, rather than that of the researcher. There are also occasions where the researcher does not ask very searching questions because they appreciate that it will ultimately be necessary for them to leave their researcher role behind, and to return to being a normal member of staff. The result may be that the ethnographic account produced is not as analytic as that produced by an outsider researcher.

A particular variety of ethnography is where the researcher turns the investigative spotlight on themselves. Instead of 'researching' a group of respondents, the researchers investigate themselves and their relationship with the surrounding culture. This process is usually termed *auto-ethnography*, with the prefix 'auto' referring to a study of the self. In this kind of study, the researcher adopts a self-reflective stance, considering the connection of their own situation with the philosophical, educational, social, religious and artistic features of society at large. A discussion of auto-ethnography is contained in Anderson (2006: 375).

This is clearly not an easy goal to achieve. Researchers cannot rely upon forms of enquiry which try to replicate a type of scientific objectivity. There is almost inevitably a strong thread of subjectivity in this type of research. For example, a researcher may be very interested in music, and want to research the spiritual and psychological effects of listening to music. The researcher may want to consider the effects on themselves, and also on a sample of other people who are equally interested in listening to music. The researcher will need to reflect upon their own mental state in an attempt to appreciate the impact of music on the mind and state of well-being. The researcher will be able to employ interviews or life history techniques in order to collect data from members of the external sample, but this will not be possible with *self-reflection*. The process of auto-ethnography is inevitably subjective, attempting to record changes in the mental states of the researcher but with all the limitations that this imposes.

Case study 9.1

If you were interested in researching the situation of postgraduate students who were working in short-term, part-time jobs in order to pay living expenses, then this might be a suitable subject for an auto-ethnography. If you too were living this form of lifestyle, then you would be able to reflect on your own situation and relate this to the situation of fellow students in your sample.

Auto-ethnography is not concerned with scientific analysis, nor with the testing of theories. In an inductive way, the process may generate social theory, but the method produces types of subjective accounts rather than any precise causal relationships. Neither does auto-ethnography regard the researcher as separate from the external sample. The process does not conceive of the researcher as an external entity collecting data from others in an impartial and objective manner. Rather it is a question of trying to understand the features of the interactive world which exists between the researcher and the surrounding cultural world.

Auto-ethnography is a suitable research approach for a situation in which the researcher has undertaken a particular experience and wishes to understand that experience through the perceptions of others. Such experiences may include having attended a particular type of school, having played a particular sport, having travelled to a particular country or having experienced a particular form of disability. One can also imagine the positive features of this type of research in that it may well illuminate some features of an experience which may normally remain hidden from those who have not experienced it. In that context, it is worth noting that auto-ethnography does not accept the conventional approaches to research, but provides a very different research strategy which can be used to address issues which are less susceptible to conventional approaches.

Participant observation in ethnography

Some researchers strive to be intimately involved in the social relations of the group being studied as part of an ethnography. As such, the researchers are aspiring to be full participants in the group, and to be regarded as participant observers. This attempt to be a fully participant observer does, however, raise questions as to whether the researcher is regarded as primarily a group member or as primarily a researcher. There is also the issue of whether the group as a whole fully understands the role of a field researcher. It might also be argued that in order to be an ethnographer, one has, to a certain extent, to be a participant; and that the very act of being a participant alters to some extent the social ecology of the group. On the other hand, some argue that it is possible to be a non-participant observer. Such a researcher would stand back from the group and attempt to record the social interactions without actually trying to be a group member. Again, some may argue that sustaining a clear distinction between researcher and group members is not actually possible, because the very act of observation involves at least some degree of participation.

It could be argued that in ethnography there is no absolute distinction between participant and non-participant observation. Some might argue that the two terms are in effect two extremes between which exist a variety of different shades of approach.

If you wish to conduct ethnographic research as a complete observer, it does raise the question of the kind of strategy you will use to be accepted by the group. It will be easier if you possess a legitimate reason to be accepted as part of the group, but if not, you will need to develop a strategy in order to be accepted. In some cases, this may create very difficult ethical situations. For example, if you wanted to conduct an ethnography of a gang of young people who were sometimes involved in illegal activity, you would probably not wish to engage in such activity in order to be accepted. In such cases, for both ethical and legal reasons, a form of non-participant observation might be more appropriate.

In some cases where researchers aspire to be fully absorbed into the research group, there is the danger that they abandon some features of their own culture, world-view and moral framework in order to be accepted into the research group. Researchers need to be aware of the possibility of this occurring and to decide in advance the limits to which they are prepared to be involved.

Sensitivity and access to 'the field'

In ethnographic research we tend to refer to '*the field*' as being the social context in which the respondents operate on a daily basis. As with all social situations, the people who normally live their lives within it can tend to be defensive and protective about that situation. They may be suspicious of people they perceive as intruders. Even more so, they may appoint, formally or informally, people with the specific role of governing entry to the social context or 'field'. In both research terms and in everyday language, such a person is often known as a *gatekeeper*.

When researchers are planning their research strategy, it is important that they identify the relevant gatekeepers and obtain permission to 'enter the field'. It is worth remembering that in a sense, an ethnographer is an intruder, and may disrupt or have a generally negative effect upon the field. It is not in your interests as a researcher to disturb the social ecology of the field. You need, therefore, to be sensitive to the social balance of the field, and to try to maintain the inter-personal equilibrium.

Research fields exist in many different forms. In a high school, one can imagine a particular class and its base room as a research field. The students will almost certainly be protective of what they regard as their social space. If you as researcher wished to enter their space, then in practical terms you would need the tacit approval of the students. Another example of a research field would be a public park. Although at first sight this may not appear to be a research or social 'field', in effect, many different forms of interaction would typically take place there. Groups of students may meet for cricket matches; parents may play with their children; personal trainers may exercise with their clients; volunteer gardeners may plant saplings; and ornithologists may spot birds. One of the interesting aspects of ethnography is that the apparently most ordinary of activities can yield interesting social interactions, all leading to a vibrant social community. Ethnography often identifies unusual events within apparently normal circumstances.

One of the problems with collecting ethnographic data in a public place is the issue of whether it is legitimate to photograph people clandestinely. Photographic data is an important element in ethnographic accounts, and yet it can seem ethically questionable to collect such data without informing the subjects of the photographs. This is even more so when children are involved. This raises the question of whether permission should be obtained, and also at what age young people should be considered capable of giving their permission, in a legal sense or otherwise.

Finally, if a researcher simply walks up to someone and asks them to take part in providing research data, the question arises whether this is an intrusion, and is putting people under a form of stress. We may consider that people have a right to relax in their local environment without being intruded upon to provide data in order to help someone with their thesis.

Data collection

One of the most stimulating aspects of ethnography for the student or researcher is the wide variety of types of data which are available for a thesis. These range from documents, interview records, films, photographs, diagrams, maps, artefacts, cultural objects, music and observational notes. It should also be noted that quantitative data can usefully be added to an ethnographic study, for example, to illustrate the range of sampling used. This varied data provides an opportunity to check the validity of the data you have collected. For example, if you have made a number of detailed observations, and formed conclusions about an issue, you may be able to verify or consolidate these opinions by collecting further data in the form of, say, interviews. This triangulation of data is made possible by the richness and variation in the ethnographic data. Equally, you may analyse documentary data and cross-check this against film and photographic material. Not only does this strategy provide a *validity check*, but it may suggest further methodological strategies for investigating your research topic.

Advice for students 9.2

When you are designing the research for your postgraduate thesis, it is important that the methodology is appropriate for the research question. If you formulate research questions which can be addressed through an ethnographic analysis, the wide scope of data types in an ethnographic study has the potential to give you a number of advantages. Multiple types of data are available to you; some of the data can be easy to collect; and the richness of the data can make for an interesting thesis.

However, it is worth noting that the very profusion of ethnographic data on a specific topic may in itself pose a difficulty. As a researcher you will need to be very selective in the material which you choose to analyse in order to investigate a specific topic. On the other hand, there is an advantage in that the remaining data may be used to analyse other issues, some of which you perhaps did not envisage when you started your research. Ethnography also has the capacity to use data such as archival material which was not originally amassed in order to be employed for this type of research purpose. Such archival data has the advantage of not having any effect upon the social group being researched. In other words, there is an absence of reactivity.

Exploring cultures and social practices

The investigation of cultures, whether or not we are part of them, and the description and analysis of social customs within those cultures, are at the heart of the ethnographic process. Although this can be achieved to some extent by the researcher acting as an external observer, the process is generally more effective in a situation where the researcher is part of the social group and can describe the social customs as an internal member. It is worth remembering that in the earlier days of anthropology the research process tended to focus upon small communities and societies in places fairly distant from Europe, often in the Far East. In the mid-twentieth century, however, attention gradually moved to European cultures and societies, and the manner in which they functioned.

Where the researcher acts as an internal member of the group, this is usually known as an '*emic*' approach and seeks to convey the social world from the perspective of a social participant. Emic approaches to social research, and to ethnography in particular, are predominantly qualitative in nature, and seek to adopt and articulate a member's perspective upon the social world. The alternative approach is termed the '*etic*' approach, and attempts to analyse the social culture from the perspective of an impartial, external observer. Such research is normally more quantitative in nature, and seeks to test social theory by analysing data within a more traditional, scientific perspective.

Whatever the particular orientation of the research, one of the indicators of a sound ethnographic study is that the account possesses what is often termed *ecological validity*. The latter is the situation in which the results from the ethnographic study are similar to the results obtained from studies of comparable situations in the wider world. For further information on ecological validity, see Schmuckler (2001: 421).

Other terms which are used in the context of studying cultures and social practices are *nomothetic* methods and *idiographic* methods. Nomothetic methods and etic approaches are closely related, signifying research involving an external researcher who typically collects quantitative data and uses it to test theoretical positions. On the other hand, idiographic methods or emic approaches tend to be adopted for research which is conducted internally to a social group, and which focuses largely upon qualitative methods.

Critical ethnography

For some people, the richness of the description of culture and social groups provided by ethnography furnishes only a partial picture of the social world. They argue that all social groups, whether large or small, exist in complex relationships with the remainder of society, and in order to truly understand the social world, one needs to examine and analyse these relationships. Moreover, these societal relationships reflect many aspects of the interconnections in society such as the differences of power and influence, the effects of race and gender on society, and the inequalities in terms of social opportunity which affect people's lives. These factors cause some to argue that ethnographies should seek to expose these factors in society, and even more so should seek to change them for the better, in order to try to create a fairer and more just society. This capacity to act as a change agent, some would argue, is fundamental to the role of the ethnographer. They also point out that within all social groups, including those studied for ethnographic purposes, exist a range of moral, political and economic values which may not be overtly discussed, but which nevertheless have an influence upon society. It is, some would argue, an important element of the role of the ethnographer to expose and analyse such value systems. Perspectives such as these which seek to explore and transform society, rather than to produce a more neutral description, are known as *critical ethnography*. For further discussion, see Bransford (2006: 177).

This form of ethnography attempts to draw the attention of participants to the types of power which are prevalent in their social milieu, and to both challenge this themselves, and also to encourage participants to challenge it. Participants do not necessarily appreciate that they are subject to the influences of power, and critical ethnography can help them understand some aspects of the exercise of power.

Case study 9.2

If you would like to conduct ethnographic research of a part of a large business organization, then the research participants may be aware of the exercise of power and authority within their organization, but they may not fully appreciate how that power is created and employed. They may not fully appreciate the ways in which authority is exercised behind the scenes. This would be a suitable subject for a critical ethnography study, although depending upon whether you were a participant or non-participant observer, the study would require considerably delicate handling.

A further function of critical ethnography is that it brings to the forefront types of knowledge, ways of understanding, styles of learning and forms of curriculum which are not necessarily part of mainstream, conventional learning. Readers of ethnographic accounts are encouraged to see these non-conventional types of knowledge as equally valid as traditional knowledge. In the original types of anthropological enquiry, respondents tended to view the social customs of distant communities as inferior to those of Europe. However, there was a gradual transition which gave more and more substance to less conventional practices. Finally, there developed a more relativistic approach which saw social perspectives in general, not as superior or inferior, one to another, but merely as different. This relativistic model was then transferred to ethnographic studies of, say, different social class groups in a European context.

Critical ethnography can therefore act as an agent of change, particularly in the context of those who exist at the limits of conventional society. By drawing attention to life at the margins of society, critical ethnography can draw the attention of governments and other agencies to those excluded from opportunities in the wider society.

Learning content

In this chapter you should have become familiar with the following ideas:

- anthropology
- auto-ethnography
- critical ethnography
- cultural relativism
- ecological validity
- emic
- ethnocentrism
- ethnography
- etic
- gatekeeper
- holism
- idiographic
- nomothetic
- participant observation
- self-reflection
- teacher-researcher
- the field
- validity check

Chapter **10**

Life history, oral history and autobiographical research

Chapter summary
This chapter will explore the way in which different types of personal accounts can be employed as research data. The data may consist of previously written accounts such as autobiographies or diaries, or it may comprise data which has been specifically collected through interviews or recordings. The chapter concludes with an analysis of the extent to which personalized accounts can be used to generalize to broader contexts.

The interviewee-centred approach

Of all the data collection methods used in qualitative research, the interview is probably the most popular. This is particularly so in the case of *life history* and *oral history* research, but also in a slightly different way in autobiographical research. Life history research is very much concerned with the creation of an account of the life of an individual person, and of linking this life study with an exploration of the connections between the individual studied and the social context of the world during the development of this life. Typically, the researcher conducts a series of interviews with the person whose life is being studied, establishing first of all the course of the person's life, followed by an appreciation of the connections between the person and the way in which the social world evolved around the person. The creation of the life history of a person is thus a complex undertaking which demands an understanding, on the part of the researcher, of a number of different disciplines such as politics, the arts, economics and history. This *multi-disciplinary approach* enables the researcher to produce a complex account which links together the full range of societal developments which have taken place during the person's life. Further details of life history research can be found in Lewis (2008: 560).

On the other hand, oral history may be seen as a type of life history, but on a more limited scale. Oral history still uses interviews, but it tends to concentrate on the respondent's account of a key event, which the respondent experienced during their lifetime. History is very often defined and described by those who have the influence to produce a definitive account of events. Oral history, on the other hand, provides the opportunity for the respondent to generate their own account of the circumstances of events. The respondents are typically interviewed about events at which they were present, and invited to provide their own interpretation of the event. This may be used as a comparison with the 'official' account provided by the more influential people who were present. A discussion of the use of oral history interviews is provided in Yow (2015: 10).

Case study 10.1

Let us suppose that as a researcher you wished to document the experiences of people who were in their teenage years during the late 1960s. This was the period of the so-called 1960s counter-culture. In the popular imagination this period was associated with rock music, drug-taking, non-conformity, challenges to the political status quo and rebellion in particular against the Vietnam War. However, you are particularly interested in whether this received wisdom about the period applied to the majority of young people and, if not, to examine alternative perceptions of the time. In the sense that this research idea sets out to examine a specific historical period, the term oral history could legitimately be applied to this research.

Finally, autobiographical research involves the preparation of the life account of someone, written by themselves, but frequently enhanced by the addition of material provided by others. This additional material may very often be obtained by the use of interviews, and may provide material which may be triangulated with the account of the principal respondent, thus increasing the validity of the account.

The purpose of the interviewer or researcher in a life history study is to encourage the interviewee to identify the significant moments in their own lives, and to relate these to the wider society. The researcher should reflect upon the idea that all human beings exist in a wider society, which continually exerts an influence upon us. The researcher should encourage the interviewee to recount their own story, and in so doing to select the events, moments and circumstances which are especially significant in forming that story. If possible, the researcher should ask the interviewee to analyse and reflect upon the reasons for a particular event becoming especially important in their own lives.

The reasons for selecting a particular event as significant may be various. Sometimes people have experienced very traumatic events in their lives and yet managed to overcome them and build a new life. The interviewee may look back on a period in their lives which represents a lifestyle or social existence which has largely disappeared, and seems worthy of being documented. On other occasions, the interviewee may reflect upon events which illustrate the exercise of power in their lives, in a way which has now disappeared. For example, in the past, where social class was a much more significant feature of society, members of the upper classes could exercise authority in a way which is scarcely seen today.

With regard to the use of interviews in oral history studies, countless numbers of people through the ages have been unable to record their views, attitudes and opinions, simply because they had no influence in society. One of the great strengths of the oral history interview is that it now enables people who are disenfranchised to have a say about events they have witnessed in their lives. Aspects of the development of oral history are discussed in Webster (2016: 256).

The great strength of such accounts is that they record the values and opinions of those who had, through no fault of their own, existed on the margins of power and influence in society. People who lead relatively straightforward and conventional lives were able to write extraordinary accounts of events in the past. This was an activity in which the individual, who until now had been excluded from history, could now contribute accounts which were as significant as those of the professional scholar.

Of course, as with all forms of data collection, the interview has its potential failings. Some events may be so traumatic for the interviewee that they simply feel unable to recount them. One thinks perhaps of periods of great suffering. For some interviewees there will be events which it is simply too difficult or too stressful to recount. Sometimes events are so complex and so traumatic that we put them to the back of our consciousness and cannot bring ourselves to explain them. For other events our memories are unable to give an account of them simply because they occurred too long ago, or because at the time we could not make sense of them, and still find it difficult to develop a rational account of the circumstances.

The essence of the interview in life history and oral history is that it involves the interviewee in selecting the most relevant and salient facets of their lives and developing these into a form of story. There are difficult choices to be made here, but ones which provide an account of the significance and importance of particular events in people's lives.

The nature of the interview is that this process is extremely time-consuming, if done properly. It demands periods of intense reflection designed to understand the significance of some events in one's life, and the lack of significance of others. Above all, though, the significance of the interview method is that it provides a medium through which we can begin to appreciate the way in which we attach meaning to the events of human existence.

Individual views of historical events

The traditional view of historical accounts was that they were substantiated by empirical evidence based upon documents and careful objective analysis. However, such evidence has the important flaw that it has survived at least partly because it derived from people who had the authority to ensure its very survival. There is thus an argument for the view that historical evidence and analysis are by their nature largely subjective. Certainly, this is the view levelled at oral, historical evidence, and used to claim that oral history may exhibit bias. The argument for oral history, however, is that although it is subjective, it does recount the lived experience of historical events. People who live through a period of war, for example, may each experience very different events. Some may experience violent conflict, while others may never see any deaths. Each person's account will be valid and accurate within its own terms, although clearly one might argue that the recounted experience is fundamentally subjective.

Advice for students 10.1

Should you decide to conduct a research project using an oral history approach, it is important to try to justify in advance your methodological decisions. For example, when you have written your thesis and are awaiting the viva voce examination, you should try to anticipate the more sceptical questions which the examiners may ask. They may argue, for example, that everyone's historical account of an event will be different, and how can you justify one personal account as being more valid than another? One possible defence against this argument is to accept that in a sense it is true, but that does not negate the value of personal accounts. Each account sheds a separate light upon the nature of events in the past, and is thus valid within its own terms.

Oral history can provide a counterpoint to the normally accepted view of the past. It provides a perspective in which there exist multiple viewpoints concerning previous times. The traditional view based upon documentary evidence may be partially true, but it can be contrasted with a more subjective view which is represented by individual understanding.

One may argue that there is no absolute truth in any form of historical research. According to this viewpoint, all historical data, whether conventional or from oral historical sources, should be subjected to careful analysis designed to test its truth and validity.

In oral history one is faced with the contrast between the validity of an oral account based upon evidence in the form of spoken words, and a traditional account which is in written form. There is also the issue of the intervention of the interviewer, whose questions may direct the conversation and oral evidence in a particular direction.

An important aspect of oral history is that it may offer a form of healing for the interviewee. The latter may have lived through extremely difficult events, and the opportunity to talk about them in a non-threatening environment may offer a therapeutic experience. It may help people to understand and to come to terms with what happened to them in very difficult circumstances. In retrospect, oral history also offers the opportunity to challenge a political hegemony, and to take it to task for its treatment of opposition groups. Admittedly, this may have taken place in the past, but oral history does permit people to claim justice in the present for the inadmissible behaviour of previous times.

In relation to this, it is interesting to reflect upon the way in which oral history can help to negate the perpetuation of stereotypes. One thinks, for example, of the persecution of the Jews during the Second World War. In an age where some people are seeking to deny the Holocaust, it is a salutary reminder for the few remaining Holocaust survivors to provide oral accounts of what happened in the concentration camps. This analysis of issues of such delicacy is one of the great strengths of oral history. In addition, oral history helps to complete spaces in the conventional accounts of historical events.

It is also a major function of oral history to ensure that the culture and language of a society are maintained for future students. The same applies to the maintenance of colloquial language and of community dialects. Overall, oral history helps people to interact with their own lives, and to appreciate the course of their existence.

Recording social movements

Although social movements have existed in the past, they have become a significant feature of contemporary society largely through the expansion of the means of mass communication. This has notably occurred since the end of the Second World War. As the name suggests, the purpose of a social movement is for a group of people to work together to achieve a specific social change, or alternatively to challenge a proposed social development. As examples of social movements designed to move society in a particular direction, we might consider the environmental or Green movement and the peace movement. These illustrate some of the key features of social movements. Such a movement can incorporate both formally constituted organizations, and also rather informal groupings of activists. There is a view that it is possible to re-create society along different lines, for the betterment of that society. The movement also typically represents a set of norms and values to which members of the movement are supposed to adhere, either formally or informally. Social movements are typically concerned with moral or religious issues, or those which could be described as 'political'.

Case study 10.2

Let us suppose that you wish to investigate the proposed government expansion of the transport infrastructure, such as new airport runways, new motorways and new rail lines, and the consequences of these developments for the environment. In particular, you want to examine the functioning of social movements which set out to oppose and disrupt such developments. You could legitimately develop this research under the ambit of an environment-oriented social movement. However, in order to give your research sufficient theoretical orientation, you would need to compare your selected movement with other comparable movements.

There usually exists a specific social aim such as, for example, a change in the way society generates electric power, in order to avoid the use of fossil fuels. Movements of this type usually involve a range of social action, such as political campaigns and demonstrations. Fundamental to social movements is the belief among adherents that it is possible through committed collective action, to bring about social transformation.

Social movements are of interest in terms of the transformation of society because they indicate how people can come together to achieve a particular social end. It is, therefore, interesting in relation to oral history that we can record and document the way in which the collectivity manages to initiate change in society. Types of social action change from movement to movement, and at different periods in history. Some social movements attempt to achieve change through rational argument and consensus, while others employ forms of direct action. One of the strengths of oral history is that as a process it can reflect the ways in which individual social actors participate in the forms of community action needed to bring about change.

The use of multiple types of data

The three methodological techniques which are the subject of this chapter are well known, first, for their use of in-depth qualitative data, and, second, for the sheer variety of the data types employed. Early social science studies tended to employ quantitative methodologies within a positivist paradigm, but the first half of the twentieth century saw the rapid development of qualitative methods in sociology, and in particular the use of life history techniques. At the forefront of this initiative was the School of Sociology at the University of Chicago. The reason for Chicago being at the epicentre of this development was that it was uniquely placed in terms of its development as a city. In the mid-nineteenth century, it had a population of only about 10,000, but this rapidly expanded during the next few decades. Chicago underwent enormous industrial expansion and required large numbers of workers to service this expansion. Moreover, the majority of this workforce came from immigrant families eager to escape pogroms, persecution, racism and violence in Europe.

These immigrant groups travelled to Chicago where they found a city full of opportunity, yet a complex synthesis of cultures, languages and ethnic groups. One of the consequences of this diversity was that it stimulated the study of cultural groups in Chicago among the sociology academics of the city. The School of Sociology was not large yet its staff produced a disproportionate number of influential studies. Many of the European migrants who came to the United States came from poor rural communities, and needed to adapt to the complex urban society of Chicago. There was a great deal of social deprivation in Chicago, with immigrants working long hours in unstable work environments, and often living in insanitary and inadequate accommodation. The researchers of the School of Sociology for the most part concentrated their research on such themes as juvenile delinquency, poor living conditions and dysfunctional family life. Arguably the most celebrated study to emerge from Chicago was by Thomas, Znaniecki and Zaretsky (latest edition 1996) and entitled *The Polish Peasant in Europe and America*. This examined the way in which Polish immigrants tried to adjust to life in an alien urban environment. The research for the book used a wide variety of data, including letters, autobiographical accounts, official documents and newspaper articles. The result was a comprehensive picture of a major transition in the lives of European migrants – a study which acted as a template for many future sociological studies.

Informed consent in personal account research

Personal account research is research which involves data provided by an individual concerning an event or events which occurred in their life. In some cases, such as autobiographical research, the process involves the subject of the research engaging in personal reflections upon their own life. There may not typically be a researcher who prompts the respondent with *open-ended questions*. In a sense, the respondent or subject of the research is their own researcher.

On the other hand, oral history and life history enquiries may very often involve a researcher who, perhaps in a relatively general manner, directs the research. The researcher may prompt the respondent with open-ended questions and encourage them to reflect upon their personal experiences within the themes of the research.

In the case of autobiographical research, respondents are talking primarily about themselves and hence have control over what they wish to discuss and how they wish to comment upon issues. To that extent, informed consent issues do not arise in the normal way since the subject is in control of the research. However, autobiographical research may at times involve commenting upon other people who have been involved in events on which the respondent is reflecting. If the respondent intends to include accounts of colleagues or friends in the autobiography, then there would appear to be an ethical obligation to consult those people about what might be said about them. In other words, in terms of informed consent, they should be consulted concerning the purpose of the research, the extent of the accounts which describe their work in the *autobiography*, and, importantly, they should have an opportunity to read the final account and to correct any inaccuracies or misinterpretations of their contribution to events. The latter issue is particularly important because the autobiographer may have had lapses of memory, or suffered from inaccuracies of interpretation. In the event of disagreements between the autobiographer and people who are discussed in the accounts, then there would need to be a negotiation concerning the account which was to be accepted as accurate.

In the case of oral history or life history accounts, there is a greater probability that an external researcher will initiate the research and act as an informal interviewer with an interview schedule. In such cases it becomes the responsibility of the interviewer to obtain fully informed consent from the interviewee or respondent with regard to the research programme. Apart from the normal aspects of informed consent practice, there are specific features which are relevant to oral history and life history research. This type of research may often involve discussing sensitive aspects of one's life, personal crises, intimate relationships or close family matters. If you as the researcher and interviewer have these intentions with regard to the research, then there is a strong moral obligation upon you to inform the respondent from the beginning that you intend to explore these topics and would like the respondent's agreement. The respondent should also have the opportunity to read the final account and make alterations where necessary. In particular, the key purpose of this type of research is to explore and analyse the way in which social meanings and understandings are revealed by the research, and the interviewee should be given a final opportunity to check whether the meaning revealed by the final text is accurate.

Open-ended questioning

In areas such as life history research where the researcher is asking questions of a respondent in order to compose an account of features of their life, there are two broad questioning strategies. Closed questions involve a precise question to which there is normally only a short response, e.g., 'Do you enjoy the process of collecting data best, or of analysing it?' On the other hand, open-ended questions invite the respondent to reflect upon an issue, and give a broader, more considered response. For life history research, most researchers prefer to use open-ended questions. For example, in the question, 'When did you first become interested in sociological research?', there is an opportunity for the respondent to reflect upon a particular stage in their life.

There are usually many different ways in which a respondent can answer an open question. This is a potential advantage in that it provides an opportunity for the respondent to reflect carefully, and then to articulate their genuine emotions and attitudes. Closed questions generally do not stimulate a discussion about our more intimate emotions and feelings. Open questions, however, can often provide revealing information on the way in which the respondent developed their world-view.

Open-ended questions encourage a dialogue between researcher and respondent. Hence the researcher has the opportunity to ask the respondent to go into further detail about their responses. The fact that there are no precise answers to an open-ended question can encourage respondents to be rather more forthcoming in providing data. They may be willing to articulate their reasoning process in forming conclusions about periods in their life. In terms of collecting data, the researcher may have little optimism with regard to collecting insightful data, yet the use of open-ended questions may stimulate the respondent to develop ideas which appear radical and unusual. The discussions which result from open-ended questions also enable you as the researcher to ask further questions for clarification, and this use of questioning probes can help with elucidation of the research question.

Despite the advantages of open-ended questions, it is in principle much easier to analyse closed questions. Since the latter often rely upon responses in the form of only several alternatives, then these are relatively easily susceptible to quantitative, statistical analysis. However, such an analysis does not reveal the sophistication of information provided by open-ended questions.

Life writing

One of the undoubted difficulties for the research student in using qualitative methods is the enormous variety of terms which are employed, and the way in which these tend to overlap. As a student writing a research proposal or preparing a thesis, there can be a lot of uncertainty concerning the most appropriate term to use to describe your research. Arguably the best strategy is to select a term which has been used previously for the type of work you are doing. At least then you can argue that you are following in a certain tradition. Second, to reinforce your choice, you can define the term you have chosen, in order to be as clear as possible about the reasons for its use. It may be, of course, that different writers would place a slightly different emphasis on a particular term or concept, but the main issue is that within the context of your thesis, it is clear how you are using the term.

The concept of *life writing* is an increasingly used term both in everyday and academic circles. It is a very general term which encompasses a large variety of concepts and practices, all connected with the production of different forms of personal accounts in a written form. For a further discussion of life writing, see Keen (2016: 10).

Life histories with an emphasis on researched accounts of people's lives; oral histories which emphasize the production of alternative accounts of events which impacted on the lives of individuals; and autobiographies which summarize people's lives through personal reflective accounts, are all embraced under this broad term of life writing.

There are many other terms which are included under the broad scope of life writing. These include social commentary, journalism, essays, letters, diaries, travelogues, email exchanges, magazine articles, memoirs, blogs, reminiscences, eye-witness accounts and anthropological accounts. Very often a piece of writing does not fall neatly into just one of these categories. To take but one example, John Steinbeck's book, *Travels with Charley: In Search of America*, recounts the Nobel literature laureate's journey in 1960 around the United States in order to re-familiarize himself with the country which had been central to many of his novels (see Steinbeck, 1980). The book is partly travelogue, partly social commentary and partly reminiscences. Any analysis of the book in a thesis would need to adopt a particular line of discussion, relating this to a broader social or literary context.

An important element of life writing is that it can enhance the quality of life of the person who either produces the account, or the person who acts as the interviewer or 'researcher', and also those who listen to or read the life writing account. It can give people a more optimistic view of themselves and of others; it can help them understand the past and the place of their family in past events; and through an understanding of the lives of parents and grandparents, it can give people a more sensitive and empathetic appreciation of the present.

The use of diaries

Diaries are an increasingly popular source of qualitative data, and of personal reflective accounts on the world. Diaries, however, can take many forms, each with its own potential as research data.

Perhaps the simplest form of diary is where it is used to systematically record events, in order that the diarist does not lose track of the dates and times of occurrences. Such a record of events is not necessarily useful research data in itself, but it can be linked to more detailed methods of collecting data, such as interviews or observational data. On the other hand, records of events can be very useful data in situations where you want to note, say, the frequency of repetition of a situation. In health research, for example, it may be necessary and indeed valuable data to record the frequency of occurrence of symptoms of a condition. This can only be achieved effectively by means of a systematic record of events. The diary can also be used in similar contexts to record quantitative data such as body temperature.

One of the advantages of diaries is that it is often easier for people to write about their intimate feelings, than it is to be interviewed about them. Much depends in this situation whether the diary is only intended for the use of the diarist, or is being written with the intention of it being exposed in the public domain as research data.

Advice for students 10.2

One use of diaries in a research context is to maintain your own personal diary as you progress through your research. This is not intended necessarily to be included in the thesis, but primarily to help your thought process as you plan your research. While you are carrying out your research you will probably have many occasional thoughts about how to proceed with, say, data collection, and if you keep a daily record of these ideas, it could be of great use in later presenting your thoughts as a systematic account in your thesis.

One of the issues which faces researchers who hope to employ diaries as research data, is the strategy by which they can encourage respondents to keep diaries. Sometimes diaries are used as part of student assessment in higher education. Students may be encouraged to keep diaries during periods of practical placements. In such a case the requirement to keep a diary is part of the agreed assessment process. In other cases, the arrangements for keeping a diary would need to be agreed with the respondents or diarists in advance. See Välimäki et al. (2007: 71), for a discussion of the use of diary data.

The keeping of diaries inevitably involves decision-making and selectivity on the part of the diarist. Certain events may be included, and others excluded, from the diary. Some events may be recorded in revealing detail, while others may be described in rather circumspect language. In terms of research ethics, the researcher would need to describe in advance the style of the records required, and the respondent would need to agree to this requirement.

One advantage of the use of diaries is that the writing of such accounts can help the psychological welfare of the individual diarist. Whether or not such diaries are used as sociological data, the very act of writing them can be helpful to the diarist.

It sometimes happens that a researcher is aware that certain potential respondents have kept diaries, and they would like to avail themselves of this valuable research data. In that case complex ethical issues arise, with the researcher having an obligation in terms of informed consent to explain precisely to the respondents how their diaries would be used as data.

Finally, it is worth noting that the rapidly developing trend of social networking has raised many ethical issues about data recorded electronically. It has become very common for people to make available many aspects of their private lives on social media. The potential use of such material requires an extremely careful consideration of ethical issues and permissions, from the originators of the data.

Generalization to wider contexts

One of the main questions concerning qualitative research in general, and personal accounts in particular, is whether it is possible or indeed desirable to generalize research findings to a broader population. In the case of quantitative research, it is generally considered that *generalization* is an important aspect of the methodological procedure. In fact, the sampling procedures of quantitative research are so designed as to make it reasonably possible to generalize results from the study sample to the whole population.

In the case of qualitative research, some take the view that the debate about generalization is unnecessary. They argue that in the case of personal accounts, the data obtained is so rich and detailed that it represents self-standing insights into the research question. It does not, they would argue, require further validation by seeking to relate it to other similar contexts.

However, there are others who feel it is necessary to try to relate the research findings to a wider population. Imagine, for example, a life history study of the work of a headteacher of a large, inner city comprehensive school. When the data has been collected and analysed, one might raise the question as to whether the conclusions apply only to the headteacher who provided the data. Perhaps one might say, the conclusions are irrelevant to other headteachers. Perhaps their professional lives are totally different from that of the single respondent. Perhaps the life of the respondent is conditioned solely by the specific social context of that particular school. One strategy to explore whether generalization is a valid procedure is to ask a sample of headteachers from similar schools whether the account of the life history appears to be relevant to their situation. If so, then one may assume that the initial research is, in principle, generalizable.

A related technique would be to select a sample of headteachers, and then to construct a variety of other data collection tools, based upon the results from the original life history research. The data collection instrument could be, for example, several different types of questionnaire. If there was a degree of congruity between the life history results and the questionnaire results, then one might be justified in thinking that generalization was possible.

Learning content

In this chapter you should have become familiar with the following ideas:

- autobiography
- generalization
- life history
- life writing
- multi-disciplinary approach
- open-ended questions
- oral history
- personal account research

Chapter **11**

Symbolic interactionism and participant observation

Chapter summary

This chapter explores the perspective of symbolic interactionism and the use, in particular, of participant observation to analyse the way in which social actors make sense of the world around them. There is an analysis of the ways in which actors construct the social world and interpret the social roles of those around them. Finally, the way in which people attribute meaning to the created environment around them is explored.

Meaning and social interaction

Symbolic interactionism is a theoretical perspective which seeks to understand the way in which human beings make sense of the world and interact with each other. It was developed first in the United States and associated with the philosopher, George Herbert Mead (1863–1931). As it seeks to explore the complexities of human interaction, it employs primarily qualitative methods of enquiry. For further discussion on the work of Mead, see Stryker (2008: 16). Symbolic interactionism has gradually become one of the most influential and widely used approaches in the social sciences.

The perspective of interactionism, as its name suggests, focuses upon the way in which the personality of a human being develops and evolves through relationships with other people. There are, of course, other perspectives which seek to explain the nature of human psychology. Some seek to explain human behaviour as a function of genetic inheritance, while others focus upon the influence of large-scale social forces, such as economics, power and class. However, interactionism tends to concentrate upon the smaller-scale social influences which evolve from the way in which human beings mutually affect each other in their day-to-day lives. As an illustration, let us take an everyday example of someone owning a car. Let us assume that this is a fast sports car. At the same time let us imagine that the owner bought the car primarily because it seemed like a good bargain, and also that he thought it would be comfortable for his commute to work. He was not at all interested in the fashion element of the car, or in the impression which it might give to his friends and acquaintances.

Other people, however, tended to be very impressed by the car. They assumed that it was very expensive and that the owner must be well-off in order to afford it. They also thought it enhanced the status of the owner to have such a car. However, when they started to talk to the owner about the sports car, they gradually began to realize that it had not been as expensive as they had originally thought. They still thought that it was a very stylish car, but were no longer quite as impressed with the owner's affluence.

As his neighbours got to know the owner better, they realized that he was very proficient at car mechanics and had been able to carry out some renovation work on the car. His skill had enabled him to purchase a cheaper car, and then to improve its performance himself. The owner still accumulated status in the eyes of his neighbours but for other than the original financial reasons. In this brief example, we thus see an interaction between people, during which people's opinions of each other change, depending upon a variety of factors. The perceptions of the other alter, as a function of the dynamic relationship between them.

In this simple example we can see that the meaning associated with an object, in this case a sports car, changes as the individuals concerned in the interaction adapt their opinions of the car and of its owner. There exists a continual, organic process of defining the relationship between the car owner and his friends and neighbours. Through their interactions, the people involved in this process define and redefine their perceptions of the car and of its relationship to its owner.

Although the car is simply an object constructed of inanimate materials, such as metal, rubber and plastic, it has the capacity to create in human beings a sense of meaning. Not only that but this sense of meaning does not stay constant, but is changed and adapted as the human actors in the situation interact with each other. Each actor has the capacity to influence, amend and reconstruct the sense of meaning created by the car.

Therefore, according to interactionists, the meanings of a particular social situation are not given or defined in the abstract, but are created by human beings. Moreover, the sense of meaning also provides a sense of morality in society. For example, some people might have initially been impressed by the ability of the owner to purchase such an apparently expensive car. However, as time progressed, they began to realize that the owner had carried out a lot of the work himself, and they were subsequently impressed by his skill, hard work and application of knowledge. They perhaps saw this as more admirable than merely spending a lot of money to buy something you wanted. In other words, the process of human interaction had generated a set of meanings which placed a high ethical value on such qualities as hard work and attention to detail. The interactional process had thus created ethical principles, which, besides being relevant in this particular context, had the potential to be applied to other social contexts. Social meaning thus had the possibility of becoming generalizable.

Creation of the social world

In the previous section we have examined only a single small example of the creation and redefinition of social meaning. However, if we consider this process existing on a macro scale, between many human beings, then we get an impression of the strength of the process. By imagining this process of the creation of meaning taking place on a very wide scale, we can begin to envisage how individuals start to define a social role for themselves, and to try to reinforce that role through their actions and utterances. They try to consolidate their social role by means of the things they say to others, and by the impressions they seek to create.

The clothes which people wear are an example of this. On one level, clothes may be worn for solely functional reasons such as to cover our bodies, and to keep ourselves warm in winter, cool in summer and dry when it rains. On the other hand, clothes may be what is often referred to as a 'fashion statement'. They may be chosen and worn in order to say something to the world concerning our view of ourselves. We may wear the latest style of jeans to show that we have an artistic frame of mind, or that we are very up to date with contemporary style. In so doing we are giving signals to other people concerning our self-image, and implicitly inviting them to make contact with us, as someone with a certain fashionable approach to life.

In a variant of this, we may frequently wear sports clothes around town when we are not going to be involved in any sports activities. We may do this because we want to reinforce our self-perceived role as an athletic, sports-loving person who is habitually involved in physical activities. Again we are making a statement about ourselves, and simultaneously inviting others with similar interests to join in our social circle. In this example, sports clothes are not simply sports clothes. They are an external manifestation of our self-image, and of the ways in which we hope to interact with the world.

In both of these examples, individuals are setting out to create their own social world which links them not only with like-minded people in their immediate environment, but also potentially with others across their own country, or even internationally. This creation of a social environment can be very powerful in the world of marketing, for instance, where certain implicit values or images can be employed to sell products. Also, in the world of social media, where many thousands of individuals follow a particular person as a brand, the creation of an image may become a powerful commercial statement.

We can perhaps see here that the same feature of the social environment can be given different significance depending upon the interpretation of the people involved. It is perhaps a truism that not everyone looks at the world in the same way. A paintbrush, for example, is one of the main tools of the trade of a painter and decorator, but it may also be used by a fine artist to paint landscapes and portraits. The brush may be the same or similar, but it may be used for a different purpose.

The social world is thus far-reaching and highly complex. It is composed of a wide range of individual 'selves', each of which consists of a number of constructs which the *social actor* seeks to substantiate through interactions with others. Social actor 'A' tries to support the truth claims which he makes, while social actors 'B', 'C' and 'D' test out their perceptions of 'A', in order to check whether those perceptions are congruent with the way in which 'A' sees himself. Actor 'B' then proceeds to say something of his social world, and 'A', 'C' and 'D' articulate their vision of the veracity or otherwise of A's interpretation of the world. Of course, these processes do not take place in a linear way, but a range of people are simultaneously testing and trying out their self-concepts on others.

Symbols and role-making

The examples discussed so far of objects which may be thought of, at least partly, as social constructs, are often termed 'symbols' within the perspective of symbolic interactionism. The most common symbols, and the ones which are fundamental to human interaction, are words and language. For example, you have only to travel to a country where you have no knowledge at all of the language to realize how immediately this limits human communication and interaction. If we are hungry and want to buy, say, four small cakes, we are reduced to pointing at a cake, and holding up four fingers. This gesture becomes a symbol for wanting to buy something. If we are wanting to travel across a large foreign city, we show the taxi driver a piece of paper with our destination address written on it. In this case, the marks written on the paper are symbols for a destination. We are relying on the ability of someone we do not know to make symbolic marks which will be significant to the taxi driver. Also, in a country where we cannot speak the language, we have to rely a lot on our facial expressions to show how we feel about something. Suppose we go into a book shop to buy a magazine. We look at it and decide whether we want to buy it. If we do want it, we nod our head and offer money; but if we do not want it, we shake our head. Nodding and shaking are symbols for whether or not we want something. If we want to show politeness to somebody, we usually smile when we are trying to communicate.

Sometimes we are able to use our own language even if the actual words are not understood. For example, on a busy street we see someone about to cross the road. However, we also see a lorry approaching at high speed. In this emergency we shout out a warning in our own language. The pedestrian hears us and recognizes the sense of urgency in our voice. The pedestrian does not understand the actual words we use, but does realize immediately that we are warning them. In this case, it is the tone of our voice which is the symbol.

Hence these gestures and expressions all act as symbols for communication. In conjunction with language, they enable us to interact with other people and to give expression to our feelings about the world around us. We can, for example, express our feelings about ethical and political issues, and obtain feedback from our peers which demonstrate their feelings about the same issues. In this way, we can gradually define a role for ourselves in relation to such issues. Our peers begin to understand our position in relation to certain social issues, and recognize the role which we have decided to adopt.

Social interaction and interpretation

For symbolic interactionists, one of the most important of human qualities is the ability, and indeed wish, to attach meanings to things that we see in everyday life. For example, if you visit an art gallery, you will not only see people looking at the paintings and sculptures, but they may also be standing in pairs and small groups discussing what they think of the paintings. In order to do this, they have to look carefully at the paintings, and then try to analyse and interpret what the painting means to them. They will then be in a position to interact with others to discuss the meaning of the painting.

If we listen to such discussions, however, we will probably notice that not all the visitors to the gallery will agree with each other about the meanings to attach to the paintings. The visitors will form their own opinions, and as they exchange their views, we can see the informative nature of social interaction. The views and analyses of individuals are exchanged and combined, with the result that people gain an enhanced perception of a work of art. This process demonstrates the way in which social existence can improve the quality of understanding of social actors, and help them augment the sophistication of the meanings which they possess.

Symbolic interaction is the study of how people interpret the world, create sense out of it, understand it and restructure it in their minds. Having done this, it is the study of how they transmit their sense of meaning to other people and hence initiate an exchange of views which helps both parties to have fresh insights.

There is an almost infinite number of examples of this process taking place in everyday life. For example, imagine a crowd of supporters at a soccer match. One supporter shouts out a critical comment at a player, and almost immediately another supporter shouts out a complimentary remark. After a few further exchanges, the two supporters begin to see the players' performance from the other's point of view.

In another example, a few friends gather at a bar for a drink, and one person complains that the beer is not sufficiently cold. A discussion ensues during which the friends evaluate the beer, and compare it with beers available at other bars. There is no final conclusion, but they each get to voice their opinion.

In such situations there may or may not be a clear consensus, but the social actors at least gain practice in constructing a social environment which makes sense to them. They practise tolerance in understanding the views of others; they learn how to combine different points of view; and how to articulate their own viewpoint even when it is opposed to the views of others.

Participant observation

If you wish to use symbolic interactionism as the theoretical perspective for your research thesis, then the assumption is that you will employ some form of qualitative approach for collecting your data. The reason for this is that if you wish to explore the way in which a person tries to make sense of the world, and to attach meaning to the events and circumstances with which they are confronted, then you need to examine their thought processes in terms of a verbal explanation. In addition, besides the use of qualitative methods, it is likely that you will use some form of *participant observation*. The essential reason for this is that in order to analyse the way a person constructs their social world, you will need to get to know them well, and to immerse yourself in their thought processes. The relationship between qualitative research and interactionism is further discussed in Kotarba (2014: 415).

Advice for students 11.1

If you intend to define your research as a 'participant observation study', then it is important that from the outset you decide the extent to which you intend to be a true participant. Having decided upon the social group you are hoping to study, you need to form a judgement about the extent to which you will be accepted by the research group. It would be difficult and frustrating for you, if you discover rather belatedly that the group is unwilling to be open with you and to accept you into their more intimate discussions.

Whether you are conducting a study of a remote ethnic group or culture, or studying a nearby social group, a fundamental assumption of participant observation is that you will collect data from that group in its normal, natural context. Suppose that you wanted to conduct a study of a group of young men who habitually meet up at an 'outdoor gym' in a park, where they train on a variety of pull-up bars and other body-building equipment. You could try to interview them, and you would probably get some useful data; but to really appreciate their lifestyle and the factors which motivated them, you would almost certainly need to join in their activities and become accepted as a member of the group. You would need to train with them and discuss, for example, the reasons for their joining this informal group.

> **Case study 11.1**
>
> To take a related example, suppose that you wished to research the culture of a jogging club in a park. It is difficult to imagine that simply trying to collect data before the start of a regular 'fun run' would be an effective research method. You would probably need to take up jogging yourself and get to know a number of different participants. Only in this way would you develop a sufficiently close relationship to understand the significance of running in the lives of the participants. This could then become a viable participant observation study.

Participant observation sets out to understand a social group on a number of different levels, whether you are researching an ethnic group living in a remote area, or a cultural group which is close to where you as the researcher live. Unless you are receiving research funding to conduct anthropological research in a distant area, the likelihood is that your research will be conducted on a social group which exists in relatively close proximity. Let us imagine that you want to investigate a group of teenagers who have recently left school, but are unemployed and have not established so far any career ambitions. You will probably be interested in gathering data on such issues as the kind of language they use and the way they communicate; their social life, including the places where they meet; their values, including what they think about current social and political issues; and their relationships with their family and friends. However, only by gaining the acceptance and trust of the group will you be able to gather data of a sufficient depth and sophistication to enable you to begin to understand their social lives.

> **Advice for students 11.2**
>
> There are complex ethical issues inherent in participant observation research. Once you have made initial contact with the research group, it is important, in terms of informed consent, that you are honest about your intentions. Before consulting the group, you will need to decide whether you hope to use anything which is said as potential data, or whether you are only interested in certain types of discourse. The members of the research group will then need to be asked whether they are happy with the proposed arrangements.

The individual self

Participant observation seeks to gather data which indicates how a person constructs a set of meanings about their own life and the world in which they live. These meanings do not arise by accident, or in an *ad hoc* manner. They are the result of an effort on the part of social actors to make sense of the world, and to understand their own place in it. The role of participant observation is that through a careful empirical approach, you as the researcher can identify some of the *social meanings*.

One of the most important results of people establishing a sense of meaning concerning the world is that this continual social interaction creates a social world which has a sense of structure. The continual discussion and affirmation between individuals help to create a sense of social stability and cohesion. Symbolic interactionism tends to emphasize the role which the individual plays in this process. This perspective sees the influence of the individual as paramount in creating this sense of social cohesion. Some sociologists place an emphasis upon the larger, macro social forces in the process of establishing social stability. For example, it can be argued that when people perceive themselves as belonging to the same social class, they look to other social class members for confirmation of their role in society. Such *social solidarity* in class provides a range of meanings which helps people to make sense of their lives.

However, symbolic interactionism places a strong emphasis upon the small -scale, micro processes whereby the individual negotiates a sense of shared meaning with other social actors. It is this development of shared meaning which participant observation attempts to reveal.

Case study 11.2

Let us suppose that you are interested in researching the process whereby undergraduates studying English start to determine a career path for themselves once they graduate. You wonder whether this would be a suitable topic for a participant observation study in terms of gaining access to the group. Assuming you can contact a suitable group of students, one strategy would be to justify the research study in terms of its potential for helping future groups of undergraduates studying English. Potentially this might be a strong encouragement for students to take part.

Definition of the social environment

According to symbolic interactionists, symbols are fundamental to the social environment. The symbols can be linguistic in nature; they may be objects; or they may be signs, gestures or aesthetic creations, to name but a few. They become symbolic because social actors assign them a significant meaning. A screwdriver is a mechanical tool if you are using it to unscrew a door handle in order to repair it. However, it becomes a craft tool if you are using it to scrape a design on pottery; and it becomes a gardening implement if you are using it to make holes in the soil to plant seedlings. As you explain to another person how you would use the screwdriver, you are saying something about your interests and activities, and how you occupy your spare time. As you talk to another person about the way you use a screwdriver, you begin to exchange views on pastimes and hobbies, and develop a rapport with each other. You are beginning to create a social environment.

Symbolic interactionism developed to some extent from the philosophy of *pragmatism*. That is, human beings learn to adapt their response to their environment. They change their reaction to the objects, words and gestures they encounter, in order to create the optimum environment. Individuals thus have the capacity to structure society, acting both on their own, and also with reciprocal interactions with the people who they encounter.

Linguistic symbols possess different meanings depending upon the context. So, if someone asks a person, 'Do you fancy a trip to Paris?', the symbolic meaning depends a great deal upon the relative ages of the two people; whether they came from a similar social group; their existing relationship; and their gender and ethnic group. The meaning of this utterance may also depend upon the facial expression of the person who asked the question. This expression may also act as a symbol during inter-personal discussion.

People acting on their environment

Although, as we have discussed, people can treat objects as symbols, they may also interact with an object on a superficial level, or as an example of straightforward reality. So, a diary can be a systematic log of events, meetings and encounters, listing the times and dates when they took place. Alternatively, a diary could be a sophisticated, analytic autobiography which discusses events in detail, and relates them to other circumstances which arose contemporaneously. Symbolic interactionists would probably argue, however, that in general social actors wish to impose themselves on their world; to add something to the world as they found it; and to create a new environment which reflected elements of their vision of the world. For them, social reality is not a rigid entity, but flexible, malleable and capable of being moulded and adapted. Interactionists highlight the flexible nature of this reality, and the human desire to adapt it to their own world-view. Researchers who want to reveal something of this process often adopt participant observation as a means of exploring and analysing this on-going reconstruction of the social environment.

Learning content

In this chapter you should have become familiar with the following ideas:

- participant observation
- pragmatism
- social actor
- social meaning
- social solidarity
- symbolic interactionism

Chapter **12**

Case study research

Chapter summary
This chapter examines the selection of cases as a subject for research, and the process whereby more general conclusions can potentially be inferred from a single case. There is also an analysis of the different categories of situation and of social groups which can be considered as potential cases for research. The triangulation process whereby data obtained from different methodologies can be compared in order to generalize results is also discussed.

Characteristics of case studies

A *case study* is a detailed research study of a single person or social context. The case study researcher might employ a variety of different methods for collecting the data. What distinguishes the case study, however, is that the object of the study will generally be a single person, or a single social entity such as a social club, school classroom or committee at work. These examples are just by way of illustration. Where the object of a case study involves a group of people, those people will usually be connected in some way. For example, you might decide to research the social context of staff meetings in a high school. Although there might typically be 40 or 50 teachers in the staff meeting, they are all linked as a single entity by the fact that they teach in the same school. It would, therefore, be legitimate to use the staff meeting as the object of a case study. On the other hand, you could use the headteacher of the school as the object of a case study. For the sake of clarification, there now follow some examples of the types of subject which could be used as a case study:

- members of a sports club, such as a golf club or tennis club;
- a public library;
- a football match;

- a place of religious worship;
- behind the scenes at a supermarket.

Although these social contexts have a varying number of people involved, the individuals are all linked by a shared activity, such as borrowing books from a library, or watching a sporting event.

It is worth noting that a case study is not, strictly speaking, an example of a research methodology or of a research perspective. It does not possess necessarily a specific *theoretical orientation*. It is more typically designated by the unitary structure of the sample. In terms of data collection strategy, the case study is more often exemplified by a qualitative approach. The reason for this is that a case study sets out to provide a very detailed picture of aspects of the 'case', and this can best be provided usually in terms of qualitative data.

Advice for students 12.1

When you are designing the structure and data collection method for your thesis, and you decide to describe it as a case study, it will usually be a good idea to combine it with a particular theoretical orientation. For example, you might describe your thesis as a phenomenological case study. The term 'case study' would designate the general structure and design of the thesis, while the term 'phenomenological' would indicate the theoretical principles and data analysis procedures.

The types of data used in a case study can be very varied indeed. Although case studies tend to be principally associated with qualitative methods, it is also acceptable to include some quantitative data where this is relevant. For example, to take a topic from the previous list such as a public library, you might need to include data on the number of books, journals and computers in the library; the average number of users; and the number of staff and volunteers. In this way, you could provide an idea of the broad scale of the library.

The term 'case study' is thus used generally to describe the overall structure of a piece of research and the nature of the sample, rather than the particular theoretical perspective. As it typically uses qualitative methods and approaches, the data can include, for example, documents, interview transcripts and diaries. The way in which these are analysed will depend upon the theoretical perspective which you decide to adopt as part of the case study. The relative advantages of qualitative and quantitative approaches are discussed in Hancock and Algozzine (2017: 8).

One feature of a case study is that the research is generally *holistic* in nature. That is, you will not normally identify isolated facets of the case, and treat them independently, but you will try to investigate the ways in which these different elements fit together as a cohesive whole, and influence each other. As an illustration, let us take the example of a research study of a place of religious worship, such as a church or temple. You will possibly start your research by making contact with someone who is in a position of authority and responsibility in the church. They will be able to authorize your presence, and justify your attendance at different activities within the religious community. They will also be able to explain to you the ways in which you should conduct yourself, in order to be accepted by the ordinary members of the church. This may lead you on to an awareness of the different religious rituals of the church. Members of religious organizations are often very happy to explain their belief systems to outsiders, and to help them understand the way in which rituals reinforce those beliefs.

Most religions have some form of holy book which provides a statement of the key beliefs and doctrines of the church. Such scriptural texts act as a point of reference for the community. They are consulted in the case of disputes on doctrinal matters, and provide a sense of cohesion for the church. You will probably be provided with a copy of these scriptures, and the church members may appreciate the fact that you are interested in reading and studying the scriptures. The church may have a single deity to whom prayers are offered, and who acts as the cohesive element of the religious belief system. There will also exist a centralized building – a church, temple or meeting hall – which acts as the repository for religious objects and scriptures, and as a place of prayer and worship. This is just to mention some of the features of the church community.

In terms of writing a case study of the church, it will probably emerge from your research that each of the elements mentioned above has an effect upon other aspects of the belief system. Hence, the concept of the deity affects the content of the scriptural texts; the scriptures themselves may define the rituals of the community; the rituals develop a sense of cohesion within the church, and so on. Each aspect of the church tends to have an effect upon every other aspect. When writing a case study, therefore, it is usually important to treat the case as a unified whole, and to explore the ways in which different elements of the case influence each other.

Exploration of research questions

When you are selecting a topic for a case study, it is important that the chosen case is circumscribed in some way. If the case consists of a person, or a group of people, then the case has fairly clear limits. However, even then, it will probably be necessary to specify which aspects of the lives of the individuals you intend to include in the case study. For example, if your case consists of the professional life of a newly qualified doctor, then the fact that they play regularly at a tennis club may not be relevant to the research study.

Advice for students 12.2
If you intend to research and write a case study on an individual person or group of people, it is important from an ethical viewpoint that you explain in

advance to the person the nature of the themes you wish to explore. In this case, the respondent is likely to be more relaxed about the data collection process, and able to some extent to plan in advance what they wish to say. It is an issue of informed consent that the respondent should fully understand the nature of the research study in which they are becoming involved. It is also important that in your actual thesis, you explain how you gave the respondent advance notice about the research.

Hence, while it is important to have some idea of the potential scope of a research study, it is also necessary not to exclude the possibility of new areas of research. For example, in the case of researching the life of a newly qualified doctor, you will probably want to produce a descriptive account of their professional life, but also you may wish to explore the ways in which they go about resolving a situation which is beyond the scope of their experience and knowledge. In other words, one of the main functions of a case study is to explore the parameters of a research area in order to delineate more precisely the kind of research questions which might be suitable for further investigation.

Historically, this tended to be the way in which case studies were employed in different subject areas. In medical science, for example, a patient with a range of unusual symptoms would be made the subject of a case study, in order partly to explore how best to investigate these symptoms in the future. In social work, the life of a particular client might be explored in order to investigate how they best might be helped. Also, in educational policy where a new learning initiative is being tried out, a case study approach might be used to explore the apparent advantages and disadvantages of the new system.

Issues of sample size and generalization

Generally speaking, a case study is considered to be a single example of a research topic, with clearly specified boundaries. However, it is sometimes thought useful to investigate several examples of a research issue, which together constitute a *multiple case study*. This can have the added benefit of making it more possible to draw general conclusions from the research and to extend these conclusions to other instances of the research topic.

The principle of collecting data from one context, and then feeling sufficient confidence in extending your conclusions to other related contexts, is a fundamental feature of research. Such *generalization* is more typically associated with quantitative methods, while it is normally assumed that there are considerable problems in using the same strategy with case studies because of the small sample size.

It can be argued that a significant use of case studies is to conduct preliminary research, as a precursor to more thorough statistical work. However, there are grounds on which we may justify extrapolating findings from a very small sample of case studies to a much wider research population. Suppose that we are researching as a case study a new form of experiential learning in schools. When we have collected our data, and formulated tentative conclusions, we pass these to teachers who have employed a similar method in their schools, and ask them if the account of the case study research sounds plausible. An affirmative response would give us at least some confidence in generalizing our results to contexts which had not been directly used as part of the research project. Generalization in case studies is discussed further in Thomas (2016: 4).

Selecting samples

The fact that case studies normally involve the use of unitary or at least very small research samples, makes it particularly important to give careful thought to the selection of a research sample. There are various grounds upon which a selection of a case study can be made. Some of these have a higher degree of subjectivity than others. One of the most subjective criteria is where a particular case initiates a great deal of interest in the researcher. Suppose that you decide to conduct a case study of the life of a teacher in a high school, and for your 'case' you select a sports teacher. If the reason for this is that you had a passion for sports when you were at school yourself, then your choice clearly reflects an individual interest. Although there is clearly a strong subjective element to this choice, the fact that you have both an interest in, and knowledge of the context, helps with understanding many elements of the case study.

A knowledge of the context of a case study can be both an advantage and a disadvantage. If you intended to research a case study of someone who was brought up in your locality, and then went on to become a celebrity in their field, then your knowledge of the background in which they were reared would probably be an advantage. On the other hand, it is possible to argue that when the researcher is very familiar with the context of the case study, it can be an obstacle to perceiving some of the more complex features of the case.

Case study 12.1

In a situation where you choose a particular case study, either because you are interested in the theme of the case, or because you possess a degree of knowledge of the context, it is important to think of the most appropriate justification for your choice. You will then need to articulate this in your thesis. In the above case where you are writing about someone from your area who became a celebrity, you could justify the choice of case by pointing out that you personally attended the same primary school, were taught by at least some of the same teachers, and hence could provide a good deal of rich and detailed data.

Another basis for selecting a case study is to choose an individual or issue which in some way lies outside the mainstream of related cases. Thus, if you were carrying out a case study of an architect, you might decide, if you had the opportunity, to research the professional life of an architect who had designed very unusual buildings. The reason for doing this might be that such a study would highlight aspects of the creativity inherent in the role of architects, and enable you to collect more insightful data.

Finally, you might have the opportunity to collect data from a person, or in relation to an issue, where the case study could be defined as a 'key case'. This is analogous in many ways to the situation of a key respondent in interview or ethnographic research. The issue is that a key case is a person or situation which in some way or another reflects important concerns in connection with a research topic. A key case thus enables the researcher to collect unusual, important or very rich data in relation to an issue. Aspects of the nature of a case are discussed in Stake (1995: 2).

Triangulating data with other approaches

One of the difficulties with case study research is the relative lack of validity resulting in part from a small sample. If you are in a situation where you are collecting data from a single respondent, then there are many reasons the respondent may use as a justification for replying to your questions. The respondent may be somewhat in awe of your status as a researcher, and may therefore try to provide impressive data, which does not reflect the truth of the situation as much as it might do. The respondent may enjoy being interviewed and may extend the data-collection process unnecessarily; or the respondent may feel that being involved in the research provides them with a certain amount of status, and therefore they exaggerate their responses somewhat.

One way to challenge the potential reduction in validity of case study data is to employ other data collection approaches with the same respondents. If the results are relatively similar, then one can have some confidence in the validity of the original data. Such methodological *triangulation* provides a means of verifying the validity of data, and to some extent checking that the researcher of the case study is measuring what they think they are measuring.

Design of the research process

When we speak of the design of a piece of research, we are thinking about the totality of the research process. We are considering the title and aims of the research; the previous work which has been done on the subject, particularly if it has been documented in academic journal articles; and the process of data collection and analysis, including the overall theoretical perspective or paradigm.

If we decide that we are going to conduct some research inspired by an ethnographic perspective, or by a phenomenological approach, then it is fairly clear to the reader how we intend to proceed with the research. With a case study, however, the situation is not as clear. Certainly, we can write aims which clearly define the purpose of the research, and we can also investigate research which has been carried out previously. However, for case studies there is nothing defined in terms of the methodology to be adopted. The only general assumption is that most case studies typically employ qualitative methods, although, where appropriate, a degree of quantitative methods can also be employed. Apart from this, you would be able to employ a variety of different methods for data collection and analysis. It would be desirable, however, if there was a degree of congruity between the methods employed, as this would help you to justify the broad approach you were adopting.

When you design and then write your thesis, it is important that when your examiners read the finished product, they can recognize a strong level of coherence within it. In other words, there are clear aims at the beginning of the thesis, which lead on logically to a particular system of data collection and analysis, and end with a set of precise and clear conclusions.

Disadvantages of small group or case study research

Case study research tends to be quite popular with students, perhaps because it can appear to be straightforward and uncomplicated. On the face of it, the researcher appears to have a lot of freedom in selecting a sample, and also in analysing the data. There is, however, a potential difficulty here in that, particularly if you are a doctoral student, you need to ensure that you have reached the required academic standard. In effect, this means that your study has made an original contribution to the state of knowledge in your field, and has reached the scholarly level normally considered appropriate for doctoral research.

The apparently straightforward nature of small group and case study research can lead to a temptation to write in a descriptive manner, without any substantial degree of analysis.

Case study 12.2

Let us imagine that you decide to conduct some research in the teacher-researcher tradition, and to write a case study of an inner city high school. This would be a perfectly suitable topic for a case study, but for a postgraduate thesis you would need to avoid writing in a purely descriptive manner. Simply writing about the levels of academic achievement would not be appropriate. You would need to analyse the possible relationship between academic achievement of pupils, and, say, employment patterns of parents, or the motivation shown by the latter towards academic success.

Moreover, the attempt to analyse the factors involved in a case study offers better opportunities to generalize from your study to other comparable situations, and to generate potential social theory.

Learning content

In this chapter you should have become familiar with the following ideas:

- case study
- generalization
- holism
- key case
- multiple case study
- theoretical orientation
- triangulation

Chapter 13

Action research

Chapter summary
This chapter discusses the implementation of action research as a means of improving a social situation or work-based context. In particular, it explores the involvement of social actors in the actual research process. The chapter also examines the cyclical process involving the reflection on the research process and the creation of knowledge.

Action as a knowledge-creating process

Action research is an approach associated in particular with Kurt Lewin (1890–1947). Lewin was a psychologist who was born in what is present-day Poland, and who migrated to the United States in the 1930s. He formulated a particular approach to research which was very practical, and was designed to change and improve society. It has been especially used in the fields of education, and in social and community work. Lewin's conception of action research involved a series of logical steps designed to improve a specific problematic area of society, through a process of planned action. Hence the term 'action research'.

The first stage in the process is to identify a problematic issue or question, which is potentially capable of being improved. It also helps if this issue is widely acknowledged and understood in the organization in which it takes place or exists. If this is the case, then people who are aware of the issue can help with the data collection inherent in the process. An example of a potential issue for an action research investigation would be the following.

Imagine that in a workplace or organization, there has been a problem with developing a policy for working at home under certain circumstances. At the moment there seems to be a good deal of ambiguity caused by employees not being clear about when permission is required, and when they may decide for themselves when it is appropriate to work at home. This has become a problem because it has created a sense of uncertainty among the workforce.

This is a suitable issue for investigation by action research for a number of reasons. First, it is a work-based, practical problem which affects a large number of people. These people could in principle assist in the collection of data. For example, they could reflect upon the advantages and disadvantages of home working, in comparison with spending a whole day in the office. The data which they provide could help in the formulation of a research plan for the collection of further data. One of the features of action research is that people who are affected by the research issue often help with the collection of data. This helps to create a democratic approach to the research process. The research by participants also helps to define the research problem in a more precise way. The research plan enables the researchers to conduct the first tangible process of data collection with a view to amending the institutional process for home working. This might involve, for example, the completion at the beginning of the working week of a proforma predicting when the employee will work at home during that week, and when they will be in the office. The proforma will need to be signed by the employee's line manager. This process will then be evaluated, and decisions taken as to its advantages and shortcomings. Depending upon this evaluation, a revised plan will be formulated, perhaps asking the employee to add further details to the proforma, such as what goals it is anticipated that employees will achieve in the period at home and also in the office.

Further data will then be collected in order to evaluate and analyse the new proforma. This plan will be evaluated and subsequently a third amended plan will be developed. This sequence of events summarizes the basic structure and purpose of action research. It is, in short, a research process which sets out to improve a particular social issue or work-located problem, by dramatically collecting data in order to initiate social change.

Action research is very much based upon the collection of empirical data, and the subsequent adaptation of the research question. The 'action' of action research rests on the collection of data to both define the research question, and then to formulate a research strategy to improve the situation. This process has the effect of amassing knowledge and understanding of an issue through a cycle of continuous reflection and revision of data collected on an issue.

The democratic tradition of action research is very important. In the past, research studies have often been controlled by professional researchers who took all the key decisions in relation to the design, planning and data collection. Action research, on the other hand, sets out to involve as many people as possible in research planning, so that there exists a process of genuine experiential learning.

In the case of the study of home working, as many employees as possible can contribute to the developing policy, and thus feel truly involved in the research process. A corollary of this is that they do not tend to feel that they are being manipulated by their work organization, but are genuinely party to the decisions being taken. The knowledge that is generated in action research is thus more frequently shared knowledge, to which many employees have contributed.

Advice for students 13.1

If you intend to conduct a research study employing an action research perspective, then it would be desirable to select an issue which is capable of significant social change. By the end of your research, you will hope to demonstrate that your research has brought about change which is capable of helping other people. You should also select an issue which involves a number of other people, in order that you can potentially enlist their help in collecting data and increasing the democratic elements of your research. It would in addition be desirable if your research issue was a practical, work-based issue, in order that there could be positive benefits for a variety of people.

It is worth noting that the action research method is sometimes presented as a cyclic or spiral sequence of events. However, this is better not understood as a rigid process, but rather as a process consisting of several principles. These are, in general:

1 the identification of a research question;
2 the clarification of the latter through collection of data;
3 planning and execution of action to improve the situation;
4 analysis of the situation; creation of a revised plan;
5 then further action to test this plan.

The result should be gradually improving research knowledge, and the enhancement of the original research question.

Ultimately, action research concerns the process of the creation, and on the other hand, the sharing, of social knowledge and understanding.

Case study 13.1

An example of a study which could potentially use an action research approach is as follows. Imagine the case in a sixth-form college where the teacher of English Literature uses student focus groups as a method of learning about a novel, rather than giving lectures on the book. The approach could be somewhat problematic because of the need to ensure that the students perform well in their final assessments. An action research approach could explore the extent to which the focus group is a valid and practicable method of learning.

Participatory action research

Participatory action research is a type of action research which places great emphasis upon the concept of 'participation'. In this context, participation refers to the collaboration between the lead researcher of an investigation, and the many people who are either affected by, or involved in, the main question which is the subject of the study. In this variant of action research, the main researcher and the potentially large number of participants work together in a democratic manner to improve a social situation. In this type of research, the emphasis is less on finding the solution to a problem, or on developing a hypothesis or theory. The emphasis is much more upon improving a situation, or developing strategies which can help the participants (see MacDonald, 2012: 36).

The second word, 'action', in participatory action research points to the repeated efforts on the part of the researchers to adapt and improve the research context. This is seldom a single process which produces the required changes, but a gradual sequence of events designed to produce positive developments in the situation. By amending things little by little, there is also the possibility of the researchers being able to reflect upon the subject of the research, and to develop more and more improvements.

The third word, 'research', at the end of the term suggests a slightly different approach to research than in the positivist perspective, for example. There is no intent to develop a hypothesis which can be tested. The approach is designed to reflect upon ways of improving a research situation. In fact, the advocates of action research try to develop groups of individuals who can work together as research teams.

Advice for students 13.2

If you would like to develop a research study using the perspective of participatory action research, then it would be desirable to identify a research topic where the social issue in question involves a reasonably large number of people who are affected by the issue. In this case you should be able to enlist the help of a substantial number of people with aspects of data collection and analysis. In your thesis, you will be able to argue that your study is genuinely participative.

There are connections between this approach and the work of the Brazilian educator and activist Paulo Freire (1921–1997). He devoted much of his life to trying to improve literacy levels among the poor and impoverished peoples of South America. Freire was particularly concerned that the people he was trying to help should be as involved as possible in their own self-improvement. He felt that through this type of participation, there would be a better opportunity for them to regain a sense of their self-worth. Discussion of his work in raising literacy levels of the poor can be found in Freire (2007).

One of Freire's key concepts was that of *critical pedagogy*. The term 'critical' points to the realization that teaching, in whatever context, is rarely, if ever, an impartial and value-free activity. It is fairly clear that when teaching politics or religion, it is very difficult to dissociate what one is teaching from a particular ideology or world-view. In other discipline areas the teacher has to make decisions about the curriculum, about which teaching materials are seen as acceptable, and perhaps about forms of assessment. The teacher may deliberately or inadvertently transmit value judgements, historical perspectives, or interpretations of scientific theories such as evolution. According to Freire, knowledge of the world is seldom independent of its context.

For Freire, one of the key facets of traditional education was that it involved the '*banking*' of information and knowledge (see Rhoads et al., 2013: 97). The pupil or student was seen as a recipient of knowledge. They were expected to absorb the knowledge 'deposited' in them by their teachers and lecturers. Implicit in this model was the view that the educationalist determines what is to be considered as valid or worthwhile knowledge, and passes this on to the student. The students, for their part, must then learn how to utilize and manipulate that knowledge. Significantly, the students have little or no say in the types of knowledge which are selected to be transmitted to them. There is thus little concept of participation here between the educator and the student. For Freire, what was required was a philosophy of education in which the students shared in the decisions about the type of knowledge which they received. In this model of education, the students worked in collaboration with their teachers, sharing with them their ideas about what could be perceived as a valid curriculum. Hence, there should be, according to Freire, no distinctions of power between teachers and students.

A key concept for Freire was that of *critical consciousness* or *conscientization*. He hoped that the poorer members of society would be able gradually to develop the awareness which accompanied conscientization, in order that they could become aware of the contradictions which permeated society, and moreover to act in order to minimize this unfairness. Finally let it be said that the central function of both participatory action research and of conscientization is for poorer people to be able to understand the nature of society in order that they can better change the world in which they live.

Social action

One of the key characteristics of action research is that it involves a process of trying to solve or improve actual problems in the real world. In other words, it is not a research activity which is concerned with laboratory problems, or even with resolving social situations which are merely of academic interest. It is a research activity which seeks to address practical problems which are of significance to organizations, to ordinary working people, or to social or community situations. A problem may develop in an industrial organization which is dysfunctional to the operation of the company. An action research process may be used in order to try to resolve the issue. In another potential example, a group of manual workers may have some difficulty in changing careers when their jobs are threatened, because they find themselves unable to adapt to the world of information technology. A group of recently retired people may find it difficult to adapt to a world without work. Again, action research may find ways of helping with these social and community problems.

These kinds of situations are 'real' because they affect the lives of ordinary people who live their lives in social situations and among communities of people. The individuals who carry out action research are sometimes academic in background and training, but may also be people who approach the world from a particular viewpoint or ideology, and wish to change the world in a particular direction. Equally, they may be members of social or community groups who are eager to improve the circumstances in which these groups operate.

Sometimes, action research is employed as a technique for preliminary research, in order to develop a strategy for a more detailed, later study. In all cases, however, a common theme running through the practice of action research is that the key researcher does not exercise exclusive control over the design or implementation of the research study. The researcher works with the people who are affected by the situation of the theme of the study, in order to produce a collective and socially-orientated solution to the research problem.

The purpose of this collaborative venture between key researchers and the individuals who work or live within the context of the research situation being studied is the assertion that the research participants will learn more about the research context through a shared research venture which is inclusive of all people working on the research topic. This joint approach to learning is a central aspect of action research, and reflects the down-to-earth issues of the individuals involved. The central social concern of action research may be summed up as the activity of studying scientifically a social system, and then attempting to amend it to the requirements of all those concerned.

Positive change

The idea of change is absolutely central to action research. Much social science research is focused upon the notion of the acquisition of knowledge about society. Action research, however, has a very practical dimension. Certainly, action research is concerned with generating a wider understanding of a social issue, but the key idea of the approach is then to change and improve the particular social question. There is also the appreciation that it may not be possible to initiate an improvement in a situation by means of a single intervention. The initial change may not yield a significant improvement, and it may be necessary to address the problems once more with the research situation. This process of continual adaptation, reflection upon the revised issue, and then further change, may continue for some time before there is a tangible improvement in the system.

It can be argued then that practical work by research participants upon the issue under investigation may result in the acquisition of further knowledge. Furthermore, this additional knowledge may then have an effect upon practical work on the research issue. This cyclical element is a central feature of action research.

> **Case study 13.2**
>
> The long-standing tradition in secondary schools of 'physical education' has been one of competitive sports and games lessons. Gradually, however, there has been a transition, at least partially, to focus on non-competitive activities, whose purpose is physical fitness as a virtue in its own right, rather than competitive activities. The investigation of such a trend would potentially be suitable for action research, as it could address the issue of the varied needs and interests of different pupils.

Reflective practice

Reflective practice is a technique for analysing our surroundings, our workplace or our place of study in order to either extend our knowledge and understanding, or to try to change and improve aspects of it. Reflective practice is an inherent feature of action research, and has been used particularly in educational research. The starting point is to evaluate our present ways of working, and to consider whether they seem appropriate or functional. A teacher, for example, might reflect on the way homework is given to pupils, and may decide that there are ways in which the system could be improved. Alternatively, a teacher of religious studies might reflect upon the way in which different belief systems are introduced to pupils. When teaching Hinduism, for example, a teacher may reflect upon the way in which the many different deities of the religion are introduced to pupils. If pupils are brought up in a monotheistic context, it may be difficult for them to appreciate how a religion may have many different representations of the Divine.

The purpose of reflective practice then is to consider how well the current method of teaching is functioning, and whether there are areas in which improvements can be made. During the reflective process the teacher should consider such issues as whether the approach to teaching manages to achieve its aims; whether the teaching appears to be functional for the pupils; whether it is possible to adapt the teaching; and also how the pupils could be involved in potentially changing and improving the teaching.

Using reflective practice to determine an area which could in theory be amended is only the first stage of the change process. We have then to determine a mechanism by which the change could be brought about, and subsequently it will be necessary to collect data in order to assess whether the change has brought about benefits in the teaching. In other words, a new period of reflective practice will need to be initiated in order to evaluate the effectiveness of the change process. If there is not sufficient evidence that the change process has resulted in significant benefits, then the process of reflective practice will need to be repeated.

One of the major features of reflective practice as part of an action research programme in education, is that it can have the effect of significantly empowering the teacher. In other words, the teacher does not simply assume a role of transmitting a pre-designed curriculum using standard forms of pedagogy. The teacher in fact develops new forms of knowledge, and new ways of transmitting that knowledge. This enhances the professionalism of the teacher, and helps them to develop new strategies to enhance the learning experiences of their pupils.

One of the great strengths of reflective practice is that it enables teachers to work with their pupils in developing new forms of relevant knowledge, which can help to diversify the curriculum and make it more relevant to the needs of pupils. This process can act as a significant motivator for pupils, in that it broadens what is taught, and provides a tangible link between the more theoretical elements of the school curriculum and the less formal knowledge which exists in everyday life outside the school.

The learning cycle

Action research and reflective practice are linked together in a number of different ways with the ideas of learning from experience, and of initiating change in society. The concept of learning by experience, or experiential learning, has become an important theoretical perspective within many aspects of education, notably adult education. The process of experiential learning is often portrayed as a series of stages, or as a cyclical process. For this reason, the term *'experiential learning cycle'* is often employed.

A typical learning cycle has four stages. In order for effective learning to take place, there is often the assumption that the learner will complete all of the four stages in sequence. A typical learning cycle commences with observations of the world around us, which usually note some inadequacies or dysfunctions in the social context. These inadequacies typically have an adverse effect upon the social setting, and the learner tries to think of ways in which the shortcomings could be improved. This stage of the process often concerns planning, whereby the learner tries to design ways in which they could learn more about the procedure, and also change some of the methods for the better.

The second stage of the learning cycle is typically one in which the learner develops strategies in order to improve the situation which has initially been observed. Such strategies may involve, say, techniques to try to solve a practical problem, or a new way of approaching a difficult situation. Having developed new techniques for trying to resolve the initial problem situation, the learner next starts to collect data in order to evaluate the effectiveness of the new strategies. Finally, the learner moves to a period of reflection on the situation. During this stage of the cycle the learner tries to form a judgement as to whether the initial problem has been resolved, or whether further action may be required. If the situation appears to have improved to the satisfaction of those involved, then the learning cycle has been completed, at least for the moment, and no further action is required. On the other hand, if the original problem seems to some extent to remain, then the learning cycle may be repeated. The learner or researcher develops a new plan of action, and subsequently collects data in order to judge its effectiveness. After a period of reflection, the researcher then tries to judge whether the learning cycle has been effective for the moment, or whether further stages of the cycle are required.

One of the important points about an experiential learning cycle is that the learner or researcher can commence their investigation at any of the points in the cycle. For example, one could start at the reflection phase, and then proceed to the planning stage, in order to develop strategies for investigating the research context. It is not the purpose of an action research cycle or of a learning cycle, to develop testable hypotheses, but rather to investigate a social context, and to develop strategies for improving or changing that context. However, it is often a side-effect of a learning cycle that hypotheses are developed which could be tested. There are a number of different learning cycles which have been developed, although the differences between them are often not great. One of the best known is Kolb's learning cycle (Kolb, 1983).

The first stage in Kolb's process is that of having a particular social experience. This may involve reading about an issue, or studying a particular topic. It may involve discussion or interaction with other human beings; or it may involve travelling and gaining experience of other cultures. This is just a few of the wide range of possibilities. It is likely that while gaining these experiences, that the learner will identify an issue which merits further research or study. In the next stage of experiential learning the learner will reflect upon the area or issue identified in the first stage of the cycle. During this reflective process, the learner will begin to think more precisely about the selected issue, and start to develop more theoretical concepts. These concepts will then be used to develop theories and hypotheses which can be used to analyse new situations. Hence we return to the original stage of investigating new experiences.

The purpose of this experiential learning cycle is to try to analyse one of the ways in which we go about making sense of the world around us. Different formulations of this type of learning suggest ways in which human learners and researchers systematically approach the process of learning.

Learning content

In this chapter you should have become familiar with the following ideas:

- action research
- banking
- conscientization
- critical consciousness
- critical pedagogy
- experiential learning cycle
- participatory action research
- reflective practice

Chapter **14**

Feminist research

Chapter summary

This chapter explores the nature of feminist research from a variety of perspectives. An analysis is presented of the types of research subjects which are of particular relevance to women, and also of the way in which research can reveal some of the processes in society which oppress women. Feminist research is also essentially 'critical' in the sense that it explores the power structures of social situations, often resulting in the disempowerment of women. In addition, the chapter will examine the processes of research and data collection, which should be selected in ways which help both female respondents and researchers to analyse the research field from a female perspective.

Definitions of feminist research

Feminist research is a perspective in social science research which seeks to address the male domination of social research, while at the same time confronting a range of issues such as the *oppression* of women in a variety of fields, the inequalities suffered by women, and the variety of underpaid or unpaid care and voluntary work carried out by women. The feminist perspective on research also seeks to illuminate the emphasis placed on the lives of men, and the way in which male perspectives tend to influence the types of issues which are selected as the subjects of social research investigations. Feminism seeks to address the biases and assumptions derived from a patriarchal society. Discussion of the nature of feminism in the context of research is available in Aranda (2018: 2).

One of the commonest ways in which men dominate the field of social research is the fact that they define the kinds of topics which could be seen as appropriate for research. Subjects for research, which are very important to women, and which could potentially reveal important details concerning their lives and struggles, may not be considered appropriate research topics. For example, women have often been viewed historically as having the central role in the family in terms of child care and in relation to supporting elderly relatives. This has often posed almost insurmountable difficulties for them in terms of having the time and energy to develop a career. When problems have occurred in the home, there has been the assumption, particularly among male members of the family, that grandmothers, mothers and daughters will resolve the issues. Not only has this been the case in the past, but it is still largely true to this day. Men do not tend to view this situation as affecting the potential of women to become established in careers, and hence would be less likely to advocate it as the subject for research projects. This is an *androcentric* or male-dominated perspective on the world, because it emphasizes men's preoccupations as wage-earners and decision-makers in the family, at the expense of the contribution which women make in these fields. There is a great deal of potential research to be done here on the nature of women's lives, and upon the effects of traditional perceptions of the roles of women on their career aspirations and development. It is very important, for example, that when research submissions are being considered, that topics such as the lives of women, whether historically or in the contemporary world, are given the importance they deserve. Discussion of the historical development of feminist thought can be found in Dyer (2016: 11).

It can be argued that men should become more aware of such issues in research, and view them as examples of the oppression of women. It is important that men learn to reflect on such questions, and to appreciate the social mechanisms by which *gender inequality* manifests itself. This process, by which women come to take the greater share of responsibility for the social care of the extended family, is also a reflection of the distribution of power in society. While men are able to exercise exclusive decision-making functions in the family, to the detriment of women, then there will be a disproportionate allocation of power. There is a great deal of potential here for research into the selective distribution of power, and the effects which this has in terms of creating gender inequalities. The ways in which the economic oppression of women can lead to the unequal exercise of power in the family and other social contexts demand much wider research, and are an example of the kind of contribution which can be made by feminist researchers.

In order to explore more thoroughly the social lives of women, and the consequences of these for women's careers and life opportunities, it is important to note that qualitative methods are likely to be the most effective strategies. If we are going to understand and document the lives of women, both in a historical sense and in terms of the contemporary pressures upon women, then we need detailed accounts of the struggles of women to lead independent and autonomous lives. These are only likely to be obtained through such approaches as life history and autobiographical research (see Chapter 10).

It is possible to argue that quantitative methods also have a place in feminist research. For example, if we wish to discuss such themes as the gender pay gap, and the difficulties experienced by women in becoming established in the job market, then a quantitative assessment of the scale of the situation can be very useful. If we are able to collect data on the number of women, for example, who hold university professorships in comparison with the number of men who hold such positions, then this can be a very useful starting point in judging the scale of the inequalities between the sexes. However, if we are to fully appreciate the mechanisms by which men come to dominate a particular field, then we are likely to need detailed personal accounts, which tell the story of women's lives in a particular social context. Although in general terms there are no *a priori* reasons why feminist research should prioritize particular forms of data collection and analysis, it is probably true to say that qualitative methods have proved the most popular among feminist researchers.

Feminist research seeks to expose the ways in which men look at the world, and consequently how this viewpoint can have an adverse effect on the lives of women; it seeks to explore how the attitudes of *patriarchy* can result in a world which is unequal from a gendered point of view; and it also tries to document the different ways in which women seek to counteract the consequences of male *hegemony* and *domination*.

It is important to note that feminist research is not simply about documenting some of the features of gender inequalities, or even of trying to explain the ways in which these phenomena arise, but of taking a more radical and critical stance in terms of combatting inequalities. To that extent, feminist research has much in common with action research, in that it is profoundly concerned with social change, with removing the causes of inequality, and striving for a more just world. Feminist research is a policy for social transformation, and hence is a strategy for critically examining society, for striving for political change in its broadest sense, and for removing gender stereotypes from both our thought processes and our patterns of discourse. The issue of the political nature of feminist research is discussed in Letherby (2003: 4).

It can be argued that feminist research is firmly ideological in that it operates from the unshakeable conviction of the domination of society by men. Feminist research seeks to highlight the ways in which men exercise power and control over the sexual behaviour of women, and also over the ways in which women take decisions concerning reproduction. Feminism and feminist research are deeply concerned with fighting against the exploitation of women, and with mounting campaigns of support for women whenever they are in situations which are incompatible with social justice. Research into the position of women is also concerned with related issues such as racism, and in particular the concerns of women of colour.

In terms of social change, one of the main concerns of feminist research is not simply to critique the values and attitudes of men with regard to the position of women, but to change men's values. In order to achieve this, feminist research aspires to encourage men to be self-reflective, and to continually examine their attitudes towards women. From this perspective, men need to embrace feminist values, with a view to transforming the relationships between the genders, and working to create a more egalitarian society.

Traditional male roles in research

Feminists in general, and feminist researchers in particular, have done a great deal to highlight the imbalances and inequalities of the way in which research operates in universities and in commercial and industrial research organizations. They have pointed out the disproportionately low number of women engaged in research in science, engineering and technological fields in general. This has led to fewer women holding professorships in these fields, fewer women gaining major international prizes for research achievements, and fewer women being noted as leading authority figures in these fields.

One of the most important factors here may be that boys and men tend to gravitate towards disciplines which are founded upon quantitative analysis. For example, an interest in cars, mechanics, telecommunications or space travel, is based upon numerical measurement. Quantitative measurement is associated with precision, with accuracy and with the social status which is associated with science. The long-term consequence of this is that men are able to exert influence in society, through their expertise in numerical analysis. When government or society in general needs to propose arguments for a particular line of action, they will often seek to justify their opinion by pointing out the support their judgement has received from the world of science. This in turn leads to a patriarchal society where men occupy positions of authority, and are usually the ones to be consulted when a technical opinion is required.

There is something about the nature of quantitative analysis which conveys feelings of precision, authority and accuracy. This is perhaps one of the reasons for the use of statistics when it is necessary to articulate complex issues to the general public. Statistics are widely employed in explaining opinion polls, electoral results, actuarial and economic judgements, and medical findings. Much of the interpretation of such statistical data often appears to be a male preserve, with male presenters in the media interpreting tabular and graphical data. Men tend to be associated with such forms of analysis, and acquire the respect and authority which accompany such roles.

There is a sense of accuracy and finality which tends to accompany the explanation of phenomena through the medium of statistics. When someone asserts, for instance, that there has been an increase in a particular phenomenon of 6.34 per cent, this tends to inculcate a feeling of accuracy and precision. When the use of such measurement is associated with men, rather than women, then this has an impact upon the way in which men are perceived in society as *authority figures*. The use of such statistics tends to create the impression that measurements of this kind are not susceptible to being challenged, and represent a final judgement on the issue in question. All of this tends to reinforce the position of men as authority figures, and the creation of a patriarchal society.

One can think of other examples of the same phenomenon such as the analysis carried out by actuaries in the field of insurance. This kind of analysis is quantitative and statistical in nature, and is largely the preserve of men. Since actuarial analysis is at the heart of the calculation of premiums and hence the income of insurance companies, it conveys a great deal of power and authority.

Those involved in it acquire a good deal of influence within the company. In a similar way large-scale infrastructure projects, such as new motorways, railway lines, bridges and buildings depend upon quantitative analysis and numerical calculations in order to prepare for the actual construction. Such projects are important from both a practical and political viewpoint, and are also again largely a male province. Those who are able to plan and carry out such large-scale projects acquire a good deal of influence and authority.

Through this background in mathematics, engineering and the physical sciences, men have tended to acquire a dominant role where quantitative skills are needed. Women, on the other hand, although tending to be under-represented in scientific disciplines, often prefer to use the 'softer' approaches of qualitative research rather than statistical approaches. There are, of course, no hard and fast rules here, since there are many leading scientists who are female, and many men who are interested in the use of qualitative approaches. On the whole, though, men do tend to dominate in quantitative areas of research which some would regard as of higher status.

Feminist research as a change process

Feminist research has a major aspect in common with action research, and that is the fact that it is very much concerned with social change. Feminists do not simply want to identify areas of inequality in relation to gender, they also want to transform the situation. They regard society as essentially patriarchal, as being fundamentally biased against women, and in need of a root and branch transformation. Many of the issues confronting women exist on a global scale, and it is gradually being recognized that widespread political action is required in order to rectify the scale of the inequalities and abuses against women. Perspectives on feminist research and the possibility of social change are discussed in Gottfried (1996).

Advice for students 14.1

One of the cornerstones of social science research is that it seeks to investigate a topic in an objective, dispassionate and impartial way. Research seeks to eliminate traces of bias and ideological thought from the collection and analysis of the data, and from the way in which conclusions are drawn. This commitment to objectivity can be particularly difficult in areas such as religious studies, politics, and moral and ethical issues. The reason for this difficulty is that researchers may well have committed themselves to a particular belief system or ideology before they embark on their research in the same field. Thus, researchers may be committed Marxists, and then plan to conduct research for a doctorate on the impact of Marxist thought in a developing country. Another example may be researchers who, in terms of religion, are

Buddhists, and plan to conduct research on conflict in a country where one of the major political groups is affiliated to Buddhism.

Finally, to take the example of feminist research, there are no doubt a great many committed feminists who plan a research project using a feminist methodology. The difficulty is that if you are in this position, then you do not want to appear overtly biased and doctrinaire. One way to counter the situation is to make a statement near the beginning of the thesis, making it clear that, although you are a committed feminist, you have tried throughout the thesis to present a range of viewpoints in order to minimize the possibility of bias.

Some of these issues concern the rights of women in relation to reproduction, and include, for example, the rights of having access to contraceptives and to abortion. What some may regard as fundamental rights for women have been the subject of protracted political battles, for example, those supported by politicians such as Simone Veil (1927–2017) for legislative change in France in relation to abortion and contraception. Further details of the life of Simone Veil can be found in Veil (2009).

The value of social research in areas such as this is that it helps to document the kinds of inequalities which exist in society, when otherwise they could easily be overlooked, or treated in a trivial way. Research helps to document the scale of social issues, and subsequently to identify new areas of inequality which require further research. Many of the issues facing women today include social customs and patterns of behaviour which involve large-scale violence against women. Research is needed in order to document hidden practices which are offensive and cruel by any standards, and yet are the subject of attempted justifications on the grounds of their being part of historical social customs. Female genital mutilation is a case in point. Research is required first of all to bring the practice into the public domain, in order that society in general can begin to appreciate the suffering associated with it. Moreover, research is needed to document the scale of the practice. Since female genital mutilation is a largely secretive process, without systematic research, it may be difficult to collect data on the extent of the issue. Psychological research is also required on the pain and suffering, both physical and mental, which results from the procedure. In order to combat the practice and to challenge the assumption that it is necessary in society, research is required to understand the ways in which the custom is integrated into society. It is normally very difficult to challenge a practice such as this, without the support of systematic research data, which can illuminate a custom which would otherwise be hidden from society, and obscured within the scope of so-called cultural practices.

Advice for students 14.2

When planning a research study on an aspect of the treatment of women which is regarded as acceptable in one culture, but completely unacceptable in another, it may be necessary to raise the issue of cultural relativism. This

raises the complex philosophical question of whether there are cultural practices which are wrong in an absolute sense, on all occasions and at all
moments in history, or whether cultural practices are right or wrong only
within their own cultural contexts. Hence a social practice may be considered
morally acceptable in a distant part of the world, but not in western Europe.
This raises the question of whether Eurocentric values should be considered
as the criteria by which judgements should be made. Even if you feel as a
student that the moral standards of the West are more valid than those of
some other cultures, it is probably desirable to discuss this issue of moral
and cultural relativism, in the interests of rationality and objectivity.

There are many other practices which involve violence towards women, and
where the objective and rational approach of research can help to challenge them.
Domestic violence towards women is also a largely hidden phenomenon in much
the same way as female genital mutilation. Research data can do a great deal to
challenge such behaviour patterns. The Me Too movement has done a great deal
to highlight the abuse suffered by women working, for example, in the film and
television industries. In such cases the accounts of women concerning this abuse
are often greatly strengthened by the use of research data. In many parts of the
world, rape and other acts of violence against women are widespread, and need
to be challenged. Statistical data on the frequency of such events is often very
helpful in mounting a challenge, and in asserting the need for change in society.

Selection of topics for feminist research

The most effective subjects for feminist research are typically those where the
collection of data can reveal patterns of behaviour or experience which expose
features of social life which have previously not been understood. Quantitative
research can reveal patterns in society which otherwise would have been difficult to expose. Qualitative research, on the other hand, can document life experiences which reveal something of the lives of ordinary women. The great
strength of research is that it generates a body of data which can be used to
challenge even the most well-established cultural norms and values.

Topics for feminist research can be considered in broadly two categories.
First of all, there are research studies which attempt to describe features of the
lives of women. The most telling subjects for research are often those which
manage to reveal facets of women's lives which have in the past only received
scant attention. In particular, this is the case for topics which reveal features of
the oppression of women.

Case study 14.1

We live in a world where one of its most distinctive features is the migration
of peoples, often from the developing world to the industrialized world. This

often creates particular problems for women. Sometimes, it is the young men of a community who embark on a journey of migration, and women remain behind with young children. On other occasions women and children set out on an often extremely perilous journey. In either situation, there are aspects of the migratory process which affect women in particular. This could provide an opportunity for research within a feminist perspective.

The second category of research studies are those which attempt to explain the elements of causation in relation to topics from the first category. As an example, we could consider the relative position of men and women in the decision-making process in large institutions. Many of the key decisions in institutions are taken in committees and meetings of various kinds. There are a number of reasons for this, arguably one of the major factors being the need for collaborative decision-making which tends to strengthen the role of everyone involved in the process. For any given institution it would be interesting to collect data, for example, on the way women perceive the decision-making process in committees. Do they feel that men dominate the discussions? Do women feel that the decision-making processes are the province of men; and do women feel that groups of men operate as cliques to promote their personal views of the way in which decisions should be taken?

As a result of research into the feelings of women about the operation of committees, there are a number of areas of potential research into the mechanisms of decision-making. One area of possible research is the proportion of women who are appointed as chairs of various committees. The chair of a committee can exercise influence over the drawing up of the agenda, and the order in which topics may be discussed. Importantly, the chairperson can determine which topics will be discussed, and which questions will be ignored. The chair can also be very influential in supporting the appointment of *ex officio* members of a committee. There is also the very important matter of the number of women who are appointed to key committees and who therefore have the opportunity to participate in key decision-making.

An important area for research is the way in which people are appointed to committees. This can have an important effect upon the proportion of women who become members of committees. When a vacancy occurs, it can often be the case that senior figures on the committee nominate or invite someone known to them to join the group. This can be a way in which elite groups become self-perpetuating. If the elite groups are dominated by men, then this can be a way in which men rather than women predominate. There is a lot of research needed to explore the ways in which male elite groupings acquire power in institutions, at the expense of women. More descriptive data is required in terms of the numbers of women working in high status positions in institutions. However, more research is also required in order to explore the actual social mechanisms by which women may become excluded from positions of power.

Case study 14.2

One of the features of the professional lives of men is that they typically have a range of social networks in which their work and social lives overlap. Arguably these networks help them with many aspects of their employment. It can be argued that women do not have access to the same types of networks, and that this disadvantages them in their professional lives. Research studies on the effect of social networks for the employment lives of women could be useful from a feminist perspective.

Feminist research as challenging oppression and increasing empowerment

Generally speaking, the term oppression is employed to describe situations in which a social group is excluded from the provisions of mainstream society, and hence disadvantaged to a great extent. There are many examples of oppression in developing countries where indigenous or tribal groups may have their traditional lands exploited for the economic advantage of the industrialized world. One thinks here of the indigenous peoples of the Amazon basin, or of the traditional inhabitants of the Australian sub-continent. The oppression here is often one of economic oppression involving the exploitation of natural resources, and hence the impoverishment of tribal peoples. There is also the phenomenon of cultural oppression where the belief systems, philosophies, artistic practices and history of indigenous peoples are rejected as inferior or inconsequential, particularly in comparison with the culture of technologically advanced countries. Very often these forms of oppression proceed hand in hand with malnutrition, the spread of disease and other health problems. Worse still are those forms of oppression where politically or economically dominant groups in society set out to deliberately destroy an indigenous people, resulting in genocide.

Other forms of oppression include those situations where an entire sector of global society is disadvantaged. This can happen where a racial or ethnic group is disenfranchised, whether members of them live in developing countries, or in industrially more advanced countries. This is also the case with the oppression of women, where there are so many examples of the negative treatment of women in all kinds of contexts. In war zones all round the world women and girls are imprisoned, assaulted and raped, and treated generally as the proceeds of armed conflict. In many countries girls are excluded from the benefits of education, and cannot gain access to worthwhile careers. The life trajectory of many girls involves early marriage, giving birth to a large number of children, and physically hard agricultural work. In addition, many girls world-wide are reared in cultures which impose marriage upon them at a very young age, thus depriving them of part of their childhood, and also of years when they could be undergoing education and training with a view to embarking upon a career. Cultural factors and traditions can impose a terrible and indeed terrifying burden upon many girls, notably in cases such as genital mutilation.

Female oppression generally includes all situations and practices which result in women possessing fewer opportunities than men, and being judged adversely in comparison with men. In our education system, the curriculum may favour boys rather than girls, particularly in terms of the subjects studied, and also in the way students' work is assessed. Sometimes group discussions in the classroom are used as one aspect of assessment. In cases such as this, boys may well dominate the discussion and hence be awarded higher grades than the girls. This may lead to a lack of motivation on the part of girls, and self-imposed limits being placed on the subjects which they study.

There are a number of issues which relate to inequality of opportunity for women, and where these issues continue to be prominent in the news. The issue of equal pay for women has been one of contention for a number of years. Managers of large organizations will often try to avoid disclosure of the salaries of their staff, in order to prevent comparisons being made. In addition, they will sometimes claim that the jobs done by women are of less importance or are less complex than the jobs done by men, in order to justify paying women lower salaries. Apart from the issue of equal pay, there is also the question of women having fewer opportunities for career enhancement than men. This can partly result in the average pay of women in a sector or industry being considerably lower than that of men. Although there are a number of cases where women have gained or been promoted to senior positions in organizations, it remains the case that, on average, women have more limited opportunities than men. They tend to carry out more unskilled or less-skilled duties; their opinions on work issues do not tend to be asked; and they have fewer opportunities for personal, work-based development. All of these questions constitute types of oppression because they increase inequalities between men and women, and further the gap in earnings potential between the genders, to the considerable detriment of women.

One of the principal contributions which feminist research can make to the position and status of women is to increase their ability to challenge the status quo with regard to the power of men, and to enable women to take control of their own lives. When social research can describe and explain the nature of oppression, it provides the opportunity for women to challenge these processes and hence to find ways to overcome them. In most historical periods, men have been the dominant gender, exercising political and economic power, which has subverted the potential of women to influence the world in which they live. Throughout history women have struggled to be in a position to control their own lives, to exercise power and influence on an equal level to men, and to be able to take decisions in order to improve the life chances of their families. To be in such a position is often known as *empowerment*, or the ability to gain and exercise power over one's own life.

Empowerment can be achieved in a variety of ways. In some cases, charismatic women are able to challenge the male hierarchy, and bring about social change through the sheer force of their personality. In many cases, though, the most significant challenge to oppression is brought about through social protest, where a groundswell of public opinion challenges existing customs and processes. Such protest movements were influential in achieving women's suffrage, and in creating an environment in which women could participate fully in the democratic political process. Political empowerment has been one of the main factors in enabling women to control their own lives. However, despite all of the rhetoric concerning the empowerment of women, society has not achieved gender equality in such important areas as the number of female Members of Parliament, or the number of female chief executives of large corporations.

Feminist research as focusing on the position of women

Arguably, one of the most important examples of feminist research conducted since the Second World War was that by a psychology graduate of Smith College, an all-women's college in the United States. The research was carried out by Betty Friedan (1921–2006), a gifted scholar and journalist with socialist inclinations. She completed her undergraduate course in 1942, and subsequently worked primarily as a journalist. Interestingly, it was as a journalist that she gained direct experience of the way in which professional women could be treated in the period immediately after the war. She was working for a trades union publication when she became pregnant for the second time, and was subsequently sacked from her job. Some 15 years after she graduated, it was suggested to her that she conduct a questionnaire survey of graduates of Smith College to investigate the way in which young women had adjusted to their subsequent lives. Betty Friedan was particularly interested in the way that university graduates had adjusted to the life of a mother and of a housewife, and in the proportion of such young women who had managed to combine the demands of a professional career with their role as a housewife.

In fact, the research suggested that there was a high level of unhappiness and frustration among these young women. According to the stereotypical role of young women during this period, they were expected to get married, have children and subsequently devote themselves to supporting their husbands in their career. It was not considered appropriate for young women to have a professional career, and to combine this with being a housewife. The majority of young women in the survey tended to comply with the stereotype of being a mother and home-maker, and relinquishing the possibility of developing a career. According to the survey, many of the women in the sample felt unfulfilled and clinically depressed at the way in which their lives had evolved. Many of their contemporaries supported the functionalist analysis whereby women were perceived as carrying out the duty of looking after their husbands, who were seen as occupying the wage-earning role. The women in the sample, however, rejected this analysis, and felt that it was just as important for wives to have a career as for their husbands.

The results of Betty Friedan's research were subsequently published in a book entitled *The Feminine Mystique* (Friedan, 2010). It became a best-seller and one of the key texts of the developing feminist movement. It struck a chord with many of the women of the immediate post-war generation. Americans at that time appeared to have a very desirable lifestyle. It was for many a life of affluence and materialism, yet at the same time it did not necessarily fulfil the deeper needs of people. The work of Betty Friedan demonstrated that social research, and in particular feminist research, could reveal and articulate the problems of women's lives, and the kinds of stereotypical assumptions which were all too often made about women.

Learning content

In this chapter you should have become familiar with the following ideas:

- androcentric
- authority figure
- domination
- empowerment
- feminist research
- gender inequality
- hegemony
- oppression
- patriarchy

Part  IV

The analysis and presentation of qualitative data

Chapter **15**

Types of data to be analysed

Chapter summary

This chapter will discuss the range of data which is typically generated from qualitative research studies. It will examine each of the types of data, and explore ways in which the data can be categorized. The way in which different forms of data can be triangulated, in order to reveal further insights, will also be discussed.

Field notes

Field notes are typically brief summary comments which describe the essence of a situation which you are in the process of observing. Having said this, in reality, field notes come in many different shapes and sizes. It is probably worth briefly describing the sheer variety of writing which could legitimately be considered as field notes. To start with, field notes can be extremely terse, with the intention of providing skeleton notes which can be expanded upon later in the research process. Their purpose is to describe the basic features of the situation in which you find yourself as a qualitative researcher. Some researchers prefer to write longer versions of field notes, which try to describe in more detail some aspects of the research context.

Field notes can be collected in many different ways. The traditional way of course is with pen and small notebook. The things you jot down can be amplified with small sketches which can indicate the general spatial outline of the observational context. These traditional approaches can be extended by the use of mobile phone technology to record short pieces of text, brief films, photos and the interactions between people. It is also worth remembering that field notes can include recordings of direct quotes, which can be very useful as data later in your thesis. When you are making your field notes, it is a good idea to try to impose some sort of structure upon the notes. You might be looking for common themes and concepts as you develop the structure and interaction among the respondents. You may find that categories and concepts begin to emerge from your data, and also that such categories relate to some of the questions with which you started your research.

One aspect of field notes which can easily be forgotten is that researchers and respondents can work together to develop potentially very useful research ideas. You may, therefore, invite respondents to read your field notes, and to comment upon the way in which the notes reflect their view of reality.

Advice for students 15.1

One distinct advantage of involving the opinions and judgements of partici- pants in the research process is that it moves away from the situation of the researcher controlling the research process. The idea of the researcher and the respondents working together on a research project is in keeping with the spirit of qualitative research. It can also be used as a process for improving the validity of the data by cross-checking statements and observations.

In the early stage of taking field notes, there is probably a tendency to col- lect observational and descriptive data. This kind of data may be fairly easy to collect in that it may consist of such features as which respondents are engaged in conversation; the subject matter of those conversations; other kinds of social interactions; and descriptions of the social contexts such as the dwellings in which people live and the type of work in which they are engaged. As your research proceeds, however, you will almost certainly wish to move beyond straightforward description, towards a deeper understanding of the social interactions which are taking place. This more sophisticated appreciation will be reflected in your field notes. You will probably wish, for example, to try to understand the way in which a description of social interactions can potentially lead to an appreciation of the feeling and emotions harboured by respondents. As your understanding of the research context is enhanced, you will probably try to understand more about the psychological interaction between respon- dents, and this will be reflected in gradually more reflective and analytical note-taking. You will gradually develop an increasing ability to hypothesize about the kind of relationships which exist between respondents.

Your notes will probably become gradually more and more analytical, as you start to probe into possible reasons why social interactions take place in the way which they did. Importantly, you will probably start to become much more self-reflective in your notes, as you try to understand more about the way in which you have reacted to the research context. It is worth remembering that you as the researcher and observer are very much a part of the research con- text, and that your interactions with the respondents are an important element in the understanding which you develop concerning the research questions.

One of the advantages of field notes as research data is that they enable you to record subtly changing features of the research context. As interactions between research respondents change with the prevailing circumstances, the emotional quality of the research situation also changes. As you begin to understand some of the reasons for these changes, you will start to have a more sophisticated grasp of your research.

It is also worth reminding ourselves of some of the ethical issues with which we should be concerned when taking research notes. As part of the principle of informed consent, research participants should appreciate the nature of your research and should clearly give their permission for you to take research notes. In this way there will be little chance of ambiguity when you are seen to be taking notes or making recordings. It will be clear that you are conducting research.

One final function of field notes which it is worth mentioning is that they provide an aide-mémoire for further research: journal articles which you need to read and types of data which it may be necessary to collect. In short, they enable you to write memos to yourself, as reminders of future courses of action.

Diaries

The use of *diaries* as a source of qualitative data is a flexible and very practical technique. The essential idea of the use of diaries is to select a sample of respondents who are willing to maintain a personal diary on a pre-arranged subject and within certain agreed parameters. The sample may range in size from a single person to 50 or more respondents. The researcher will usually provide guidance notes or instructions on the maintenance of the diaries. These may range from giving the respondents complete autonomy in terms of the structure of the diary and with regard to the style of writing, to fairly precise guidance with respect to the questions to be addressed and the manner in which comments would be written. In the case of a highly structured diary, the researcher would probably define the time in each day when a diary entry would be made, and the approximate length of each entry. The traditional technique of maintaining a diary would involve a notebook and pencil, but modern technology has supplemented this with a variety of electronic techniques. Smartphones enable the basic text to be supplemented with photographs, copies of documents, audio and video recordings, and many other features.

Diary research is essentially a longitudinal study which investigates changes in a research context over time, or which explores the creation of new codes and concepts which emerge from the developing diary accounts. Diary research attempts to study transformations in the social setting of the research, and to examine the way in which the research issues develop over a period of time. One of the great advantages of diary research is that the respondents are able to continue working on their diaries without any particular intervention from the researcher. Once the latter has arranged the procedures and ensured that the participants understand the guidance which they have been given, then the researcher can await the submission of the data, and proceed with the analysis.

From the researcher's point of view, diary research is very time-effective, with the major investment in time being during the initial organization of the research project. The development of diary research is discussed in Hyers (2018: 2).

***

Case study 15.1

We begin to see the full value of diary research in situations where the respondents are scattered over a fairly wide geographical area. This might be in a case such as a study of college principals. Once the instructions for maintaining the diaries have been sent out to participants, the researcher can await the submission of diaries. If the researcher has any queries about a particular diary, then these can easily be taken up with the relevant respondent.

***

There are a number of other significant advantages to diary research. It can be a very useful method for collecting data on issues which are very delicate, and upon which respondents may normally be very reluctant to pronounce. If, as a researcher, we ask respondents to discuss personal matters, they may be extremely reluctant and may feel embarrassed to do this. On the other hand, respondents may feel that the writing of a diary does not really involve the same kind of interaction with a third party. Although they realize that ultimately their diary will be read by the researcher, the act of writing the diary may seem more personal and confidential, and hence the respondents may be more willing to discuss personal matters. From an ethical point of view, however, since respondents may be writing about personal issues, it is important that they appreciate fully the way in which their data will be used.

Research diaries also enable you to collect data simultaneously from a wide variety of different social contexts by asking respondents to initiate data collection at certain specific times of the day. For example, you might wish to investigate whether respondents are feeling generally optimistic or pessimistic at certain times, and as far as they can tell, why this is so. The fact that the data is being collected simultaneously, yet in different locations, may generate a variety of interesting responses.

Diaries generate data which has a strong sense of immediacy, and which has a naturalism reflecting the world as it existed at the moment in which the data was collected. Data from diaries reflects the world as perceived by the respondent at the time during which the diary was completed. The use of diaries can be very convenient for the researcher since they can in effect collect data from a wide variety of contexts, notably in whichever situation the respondent happens to be. Normally, because of the physical distance between the respondent and the researcher, the latter is not in a position to influence the data collection process, and therefore the objectivity of the data may well be increased.

There are, however, several potential disadvantages to the use of diaries in research. As the respondents are rarely subject to immediate supervision, they may develop the habit of completing their diary some time after the events which are being recorded. If respondents make their diary entries in this way, then there may be concerns about the effects of inadequate memory. Finally, in some cases, respondents may find it disconcerting to write about issues which recreate unhappy memories, particularly when they know that the researcher will read these accounts. If the researcher is aware that this kind of issue may arise, then it may be advisable to discuss it with the respondent, and develop a strategy which may minimize any difficulties for the respondent.

Biographical accounts

A *biography* is an account of the life of a person written by the researcher rather than by the person themselves. Biographies, however, are not simply a list of key dates in someone's life, with an account of notable events and achievements. A biography links the main facts of the life of someone with the social trends of the period, the main political events and other principal characters of the time, and examines the reasons for thinking of the person concerned as significant. An *autobiography*, on the other hand, is written by the person themselves, and inevitably presents a more subjective image of the life of a person. One of the main advantages of an autobiography is that the subject of the writing has detailed access to the key events of their own life. They can write about events with *subjectivity* and authority, simply because they were party to those events. On the other hand, it may be more difficult to set the person's life in context, because they are in a sense, too close to these events, and are unable to stand back and examine the social context dispassionately.

Biographies are usually written about the life of someone who has occupied a role of some significance in the world. They do not necessarily have to be well known. They could have worked in a particular field, and had a significant role to play in that field, without in fact being particularly well known outside their specialism.

It is important, however, that a biography does more than simply tell a chronological story of the life of a person. It should place that life within the main events of the period. These may be political events, social events, social or military conflicts, social change, and transformations in industrial and economic practices. As a researcher, considering embarking on a biographical account, this is where you would need to conduct wide-ranging research in order to understand the developments in the period. For example, if you were considering researching the everyday life of an individual soldier in the First World War, you would need to research the politics of the period, and how this affected decisions on the battlefield; you would need to be familiar with the kind of food supplied to troops, the weapons used, and the kind of medical supplies available. This is just to mention a few aspects of the background information required.

It is also worth being clear about the reasons for selecting this particular soldier, and importantly the nature of the data you have available. It is easy to think of potentially interesting research studies, but unless you possess a significant quantity of useful data, then it will be very difficult to write a meaningful research study. However, suppose that you have access to a large number of previously unknown letters written by this soldier to his loved ones in England, then this may open up a number of research possibilities. You may, for example, have sufficient data to be able to write a study of the amount of information concerning the battlefield which reached England via soldiers' letters.

Advice for students 15.2

It is very often the case that researchers think that the best way to proceed with a research study is to first identify a topic or subject for the research, and subsequently to start looking for data. There does appear to be a certain logic to this approach, but clearly if very little data on a subject proves to be available, then it will be very difficult indeed to conduct the research. The alternative approach is to seek out a range of potential data on a theme, and then try to evaluate in your own mind how this data might support a particular research study. This second strategy has at least the benefit of practicability. The final subject may not be ideally the one which you would choose, but there is every likelihood that you will be able to complete your study.

The question of data is very important with biographical accounts. If the subject of the research is still alive, then you will hopefully have the benefit of their support with the research. If they will help by giving of their time with interviews, then you will have the opportunity to gather significant primary data. The subject may also provide you with a variety of data such as letters, photographs, *artefacts*, manuscripts and contact details for people they have known, and who may well be willing to provide further personal information. In the case of someone who is fairly well known, there may also be a significant amount of information in books, journals and other publications. This can be cross-referenced with other data. The meticulous checking and verification of data are an important element of the writing of a research biography.

Interview transcripts

When starting to design a research study based on the use of interviews, one of the important early decisions to be taken is the size of the sample, and the people who are to be included in the sample. It is also necessary to carefully consider the justification of the inclusion of the future interviewees. This justification will need to be discussed and defended in the thesis. Even though you may take a great deal of care in the selection of interviewees, it is very difficult to predict the nature and the amount of data which each interviewee may provide for the study. Some interviewees may be by nature loquacious, and may provide very large quantities of data. Others, however, may be fairly reluctant to go into great detail about the research subject at hand. Some interviewees may have a profound interest in the research topic, and this may motivate them to make a lot of comments about the research subject. Others, however, may have relatively little interest and may keep their comments to a minimum.

At the end of the data collection phase, you will probably find that you have large amounts of recordings concerning your research. Before you can continue with the research analysis, you will need to label your interview recordings. In order to preserve the anonymity of the respondents, it is probably better not to employ the real names of the respondents. You should normally use fictional names for each respondent, and adhere to names which reflect the actual gender and cultural background of people. The next stage is to produce written transcripts from the audio recordings. One thing is likely to emerge during this stage of the process: you will almost certainly produce far more written transcripts than you imagined. There is also the question of how much proportionately you will include from each interview respondent. For example, suppose that interviewee A generates ten pages of transcripts, while interviewee B only generates half a page of transcripts. The question arises whether in the final thesis you will include 20 times more quotations from interviewee A as from interviewee B.

The other issue is whether the longer transcripts from interviewee A contain as much material of substance as the shorter transcripts from interviewee B. It may be, for example, that the data from A consists of relatively bland material, without a great deal of substance; whereas the material from B is succinct and clear, even though it is slightly brief. All of these issues have to be taken into account, as you are preparing your typed transcripts.

There are several other issues to be taken into account concerning the actual transcription process. One is the question of who will carry out the actual transcription process. One thing is certain; it can be a very time-consuming process. As the researcher, you could conduct the transcription yourself. An advantage of this is that you start to familiarize yourself with the data from an early stage, and in effect begin aspects of the analytic process. The other alternative, however, is to obtain help with the process. This may entail getting help from a friend or colleague, or indeed employing someone else.

Another aspect of the transcription process is the manner in which aspects of the spoken language of the interview are reflected in the written text of the *transcript*. For example, the interviewee may from time to time emphasize certain words or expressions, and this emphasis may have a very significant effect upon the meaning of the discourse. It is important that this emphasis is indicated in the transcript, and that there is a consistency with which such emphases are indicated. In other words, there needs to be a code or some form of diacritical mark which indicates the emphasis. This may be as simple as underlining all emphasized words or phrases, or perhaps transcribing them in bold. Another example might be when the interviewee employs the use of pauses. This could be indicated by a series of dashes or dots, each dash representing, say, 1 second of pause. It is not possible to represent the complexity of spoken language in written text, but by coding certain linguistic features, one can reproduce some of the nuances of meaning.

The next stage in the analytic process is to examine all of the transcripts, to read them very carefully, and to highlight or otherwise identify the key quotations which you feel will help to gradually construct an understanding of the research question. Let us suppose that you have interviewed a sample of school-teachers about what they regard as the most important issues in their job. As you read the first transcript, you realize that there is considerable emphasis upon the maintenance of discipline in the classroom. This seems to be the most important issue for the teacher. As you proceed to read more transcripts from other teachers, the same issue keeps arising. In this case, you feel more and more confident in placing this issue at the centre of your developing understanding. As you continue with your reading and analysis, a range of other issues arise, and you need to decide which themes may be part of your developing theory.

Once you have decided upon the main themes which emerge from your analysis of the transcripts, there are still key decisions to be taken in the ongoing analysis. One of the most important is the selection of parts of the transcript to be included in your thesis. There will simply be far too much transcript data to include everything in your thesis, and hence you will need to make a selection. Importantly, however, you will also need to explain in your thesis the rationale for making this selection. In short, you should always try to justify each methodological decision which you make.

Official documents

As a category, *official documents* include a very wide range of written material, the majority of which was probably not written to be used as research data. In the contemporary academic world, when we adopt a particular research methodology and plan carefully a strategy for collecting data, we try to embed a large number of safeguards in our procedures, in order to eliminate bias in the final data which we collect. However, these safeguards do not necessarily exist with official documents which may have been created for a diversity of reasons other than scholarship or academic enquiry.

Official documents may include draft or actual legislation; records of legal procedures; results of judicial enquiries; birth and death certificates; inheritance of titles; deeds of ownership; wills and testaments; records of purchases and sale; records of land or property sales; records of battles and conflicts; academic records; wealth and taxation records; insurance records; census and population records; records of large business corporations, government and branches of government, and academic institutions; and records of media institutions. This list is far from being exhaustive.

Case study 15.2

So complex are some of these documents that it may be quite difficult to analyse them in such a way that one can form judgements about them. These documents may be very useful in biographical research, but you will probably need to combine the data from a number of different documents in order to collate a reasonable amount of data. Overall, documents can be very useful as data sources, since they are not altered over time through the intervention of different researchers. Nevertheless, there are a number of questions which can be asked about them, not least of which is the issue of how these particular ones have survived, and not other documents.

One of the problems which exists with such documents is that it may not be possible to gain access to them easily. Large business corporations, for example, may have a wide range of documents, in both paper and electronic copies, but may not wish to release them to public scrutiny, perhaps because they reveal sensitive information about company profits, or because they contain personal information about clients. In addition, companies and organizations often reveal in their documents strategies for carrying out policy decisions, and the moral grounds upon which they take their decisions. In the contemporary world, ethical decision-making in business is a major issue, and yet ethical issues are not always clear-cut. Some organizations may prefer not to become too enmeshed in debate about these complex issues.

Official documents are also very important to the extent that they may reveal a certain amount of bias in the way in which they are written and produced. Central to this issue is the question of the person who wrote or prepared the document, and the reasons for so doing. Not all documents may be biased, of course, but one has to be circumspect in considering this possibility, and in evaluating the approach of the document writer, particularly if their identity is known.

The *objectivity* of documents is an important issue if they are being used as research data. It might not be unreasonable to suppose that if, say, a government employee produces a document such as an official report, it will be written at least partially with a view in mind to the attitude of the leading members of the government. When such documents are being interpreted as potential research data, it is important that they are read from the point of view of potential bias.

An important advantage of official documents, however, is the fact that as data, they remain constant, irrespective of the people who are inspecting them. If you imagine an interview recording, and ask several different people to transcribe it, then you would almost certainly obtain several slightly different versions of the transcript. With official documents, there is, however, only a single version of a particular document, although it is true to say that individual researchers may interpret it in different ways.

Emails and text messages

One of the main advantages of the use of *emails* and other forms of electronic messages in research is one of the organization of the research process, and the speed and efficiency with which respondents can be contacted. In the early stages of setting up a research study, one of the first issues is the establishment of a sample. If you have access to the names of a group of people and their email addresses, then it would be relatively easy to contact them all, with an explanation of the research project, and asking them if they are willing to participate. You would of course need to comply with the normally accepted standards of informed consent, and also inform people of an estimate of the work and time involved for a participant. Not all of the potential participants would normally be likely to agree to take part, but with a certain amount of good fortune you should be able to enlist the help of sufficient people to form an acceptable sample. If you have access to a circulation list for a particular profession, such as education, you may be able to distribute your request to relevant professionals. For example, if your research involved the teaching of science in high schools, you might be able to obtain the communication details of a large number of science teachers. In this case, the science teachers might consider that it was in their professional interest to take part in the research, and so would agree to be a member of the sample.

Once you have the documents about the research ready for circulation, it should be a fairly rapid process to start collecting data. There are also some practical advantages to collecting data in this way. If a respondent or respondents have some misunderstandings or queries about the research instructions, then they can contact the researcher directly for guidance. This can save a lot of time for the researcher, and also avoid research data being submitted in the wrong format.

A major advantage of email data is that the latter is already in typed format and hence there is no transcription required from audio recording to text format. In addition, when respondents furnish data in email format, they can spend a good deal of time considering their responses, and making certain that they say exactly what they want to say.

Photographs

Photographic data is a very immediate and vivid form of data. By this, I mean that *photographs* can highlight evidence which is not easy to describe with other forms of data. Imagine a research study in which the style of dress of participants is an important factor. This would not be easy to describe in written language, yet a few relevant photographs could quickly and easily portray the style of clothing worn.

It is very often the case, however, that photographs are used in a research study in combination with other forms of data. Photographs on their own may simply not provide sufficient data, and there may be gaps left in the information provided with the photograph. For example, in the case of historical photos, we may not have the basic information such as the identity of the photographer, the reasons for taking the photograph, the location of the photo, and the identities of the people in the photo. There is also the question of whether the photo was artificially designed, and did not therefore represent a real-life interaction between people.

If the photo is artificially structured, then there is the question of whether a certain amount of bias has crept into the image. For example, the photo may suggest certain levels of interaction between individuals which are not actually present in everyday life. A possible remedy for the existence of a certain degree of bias is to encourage participants to take some photographs themselves. This could go some way to removing potential bias on the part of the researcher.

One of the major issues with the taking of photographs for research purposes is that of ethical principles. For example, you may decide that for your research you would like to take some photographs of urban landscapes. Almost inevitably you would include some images of other people within the townscape. You will probably not know the identity of the people, and nor will they know you. In addition, even if they see you taking photographs, they will probably not associate it with a research project. If you wanted to try to obtain the permission and informed consent of the people who might possibly be included in the photographs, then this might be unrealistic, given that the people are probably moving around fairly rapidly in the area. The essential question is whether it is ethical to use photographs you have taken of people, without their being aware that their photo images are being used for research purposes. In a perfect world, the people involved would give their informed consent to their images being used. However, in this context it may be difficult to achieve this, and hence a different form of ethical justification may be necessary. When the photographs are being taken, if the emphasis appears to be on the built environment rather than people, and the latter tend not to be in the foreground of the photo, then you could argue that the use of photographs in ethically acceptable. Again, as we have discussed on a number of occasions, the main requirement for your thesis is that you explain the ethical grounds on which you have tried to conduct the research, and carefully articulate the basis of your justification.

Audio and video recordings

We have examined in some detail the issues involved in the use of *audio recordings*, particularly in the context of interview research. *Video recordings* combine some elements of the use of audio data, with the use of still photographs. Video recordings still need to be transcribed into written data, in order that they can be employed in your thesis. The audio element can be transcribed into textual data, while you can add notes and comments based on the video elements of the data. For example, you may be able to comment on mannerisms and gestures which appear on the video film, and which shed light on the interpretation of the textual material.

There are various adaptations of video recordings which are often used in conjunction with other types of qualitative data. The term 'videography' is often used in parallel with ethnography, to indicate qualitative data which is collected in the form of videos in a naturalistic, ethnographic setting. Sometimes in this type of research, the participants are encouraged to use the video camera themselves, in order to encourage them to film the aspects of the social setting which they themselves consider significant. This is to encourage the participants to adopt a more proactive role in the research, and not to leave the key decisions to the researcher.

Triangulation of data

When you use a single form of qualitative methodology to investigate a research topic, or a single form of data collection, there is always the possibility that a certain element of bias may affect the results. One of the commonest ways of trying to avoid this is to use two different methods to investigate the same research issue. You can then compare the results for consistency. If the two methods or data collection approaches provide fairly similar results, then this will create a certain amount of confidence in the data. *Triangulation* as a method adopts its approach from techniques in surveying. If you know the distance between two points, and the angles they make with a third point, you can use the simple geometry of a triangle to calculate the distance of that third point.

The principle of triangulation is helpful, because for any given qualitative research investigation, it is often possible to think of two data collection approaches which in principle would be appropriate. For example, in a study of the pressures on a group of psychiatric nurses, it would be possible to employ, say, informal interviews or the use of diaries. Both methods could in principle yield interesting results, which could be compared with a view to establishing the validity of both types of data.

Learning content

In this chapter you should have become familiar with the following ideas:

- artefacts
- autobiographies
- biographies
- diaries
- field notes
- objectivity
- official documents

- photographs as research
- subjectivity
- transcripts
- triangulation

Chapter 16

Grounded theory

Chapter summary
The chapter will start with an analysis of the process of inductive theory generation, comparing this with the process of theory testing. The creation of theory through induction will be analysed in terms of it being a valid scientific process. There will be an examination of the generation of concepts through the actual process of data analysis, and the gradual building of theory. In addition, the sampling of data will be discussed in relation to the gradual emergence of a theory. Where relevant, reference will be made to computer-assisted analysis packages in order to shed light on ways in which such software can speed up and enhance the data analysis process.

Social constructivism and theory generation

At the heart of qualitative research is the concept of the way in which new knowledge and understanding are generated. The basic premise of the qualitative approach to research is that knowledge is created through the process of reaction and interaction between people. In everyday life, people test out their thoughts and ideas on each other, proposing their different notions of the world. Sometimes their ideas are accepted and sometimes they are rejected, but the overall idea of *social constructivism* is that there is an interplay between individual people, which results in the acceptance of new ideas.

As the term 'social constructivism' suggests, new ideas, concepts and ways of understanding are pieced together in the form of new hypotheses and theories through a process of mutual exploration between people. New ways of looking at the world are literally built up and constructed through the process of people exploring the world together. This process is fundamentally social, in that it depends upon people discussing new ideas and possibilities about the world and coming to a consensus about a new world-view.

Suppose, for example, that you are researching the most appropriate management style for a contemporary manufacturing business. In the spirit of qualitative enquiry, and social constructivism, you would not try to test a specific hypothesis, but would explore the opinions and judgements of people working in the business. This would not only involve discussions and interviews with senior managers, but also with employees on the shop floor. The purpose of the research, within a social constructivist perspective, would be to collect data which reflected the wide range of opinions on appropriate management styles, and then to carefully distil an approach which seemed to reflect a consensus from the different range of views in the company.

The approach of social constructivism is thus one of participation, where each of the social actors is not only able to contribute to the data collection and analysis, but actually encouraged to do so. Social constructivism thus tends to open up research as an activity. Generally, it does not separate out the research process into researchers and data providers. Everyone is seen as having a distinctive perspective and contribution to make to the whole of the research enterprise. Thus, in the exploration of management styles, although shop floor workers may not, on paper, be considered experts on management, they are in fact at the receiving end of whatever approach to management prevails at the time in that organization. Shop floor workers are ideally placed to make judgements about whether a particular approach to managing personnel, or the production process, is generally supportive of sound staff relations or enhanced productivity.

The approach of social constructivism in research is thus not to predetermine who might have special insights into a particular phenomenon, but to be open-minded about who might help to create a new approach which ultimately could generate a new theory about the most helpful way to manage employees. From the point of view of constructivism, if we wish to understand the processes of personnel management, we should not restrict ourselves to reading the large set texts, which articulate the best-known theories of management. These may well be a useful starting point for our research investigations, but constructivism considers the central approach of research to involve the collection of a range of data and the subsequent analysis of this material in order to develop new systematic insights, which could form the basis of new social theory. For social constructivists, the expansion of knowledge and understanding is not viewed as a process of simply adding to existing insights, but rather as the creation of new forms of looking at the world. Constructivism is seen as a dynamic process, which furthers the development of new social theory and systematic understandings of the world.

When we are carrying out research, it is worth remembering that within a qualitative framework, both researchers and respondents approach the process of research in their own individual way. If we imagine two researchers each conducting their research using the same research design, we could not expect them to collect the same type of data, nor to analyse the data in precisely the same way. This would be the case even if they both used the same respondents, and carried out their research in the same social environment. The fundamental reason for this discrepancy is that the two researchers would have inevitably been reared in different environments and would have had different educational experiences in their lives. These fundamental differences would have meant that they asked questions in a slightly different way in interviews, and also interpreted data in a different way during analysis.

Similar differences would also have occurred if the same researcher collected data from two separate groups of respondents. Even if the respondent groups were matched as far as possible in terms of their background and attitudes, and were asked the same questions in as far as possible the same way, we could not reasonably expect the same kind of responses. In other words, research is not a predictable process. No matter how one tries to introduce a degree of certainty or comparability into research, unpredictable events will occur, created by the social backgrounds of those involved in the process. Moreover, the theories which we develop from the qualitative research process, do not depend exclusively upon the research design which we use, but also upon the complexities of the life experiences of researcher and respondents.

Grounded theory as science

The philosophical approach of constructivism is thus at the heart of the way in which we interpret qualitative data. At first sight it may seem as if the processes of analysing quantitative and qualitative data are very different. Quantitative methods involve the collection of numerical data which is used to test hypotheses with a view to articulating general statements, laws or theories. These can then be used to attempt to predict future events. Qualitative research may appear to be very different in that it employs verbal data, which, of necessity, has to be treated in a different manner to statistical, mathematical methods. Nevertheless, there are similarities between the two broad approaches, and both may in certain respects be seen as applying the same key scientific principles. Both qualitative and quantitative research involve the systematic, planned collection of data; the analysis of the data according to accepted principles; the aim of producing general statements about the world; the attempt to validate those statements, and the continual willingness to subject those statements to revision where they appear to require it.

There are, however, despite the adherence of both approaches to broad scientific principles, rather different questions of emphasis. Whereas quantitative research emphasizes the testing of hypotheses, qualitative research is concerned with the generation of theory from the data. This approach to qualitative research was particularly articulated by Glaser and Strauss (1967), who employed the term '*grounded theory*' to describe the process of developing social theory from the data which had been collected. The approach was termed grounded theory because the theory which was developed was essentially based on, or grounded in, the data which had been collected. The argument that grounded theory is fundamentally scientific is enhanced by the strategy of seeking structures and organization in the data which is collected. The grounded theory process starts by the general collection of data on a topic which attracts the researcher. As more data is collected, the researcher seeks to identify sequences and relationships in the material collected. These sequences influence the future patterns of data collection, not only to provide more detail on existing data structures, but also to suggest new areas of investigation. The overall process of data collection and analysis thus develops a type of logic which has many features of the scientific process.

Gradually, the sequences and inter-relationships of the data begin to develop into a theory, or clear, succinct statement of the connections between the data. Such a theory, if clearly grounded in the data, should begin to have a predictive capacity. That is, one should gradually begin by being able to predict and estimate the way in which existing data and the developing theory can make an estimate of the way in which future data can function. It should be remembered that no social science theory can ever be considered certain of predicting the future, and if it fails to do so, then the theory will need to be re-tested and re-applied to a fresh body of data.

A theory is generally accepted as revealing 'truth' as long as it is compatible with the data which is emerging. However, if it fails to accurately predict the future, then it is regarded as having been falsified, and will need to be amended until it more accurately fits the data.

An inductive approach to empirical analysis

One of the central problems of philosophy, and thus of research in general, is the question of how we can be certain that something is 'true'. Generally speaking, we accept the veracity of data in research when it accords with the evidence of our senses, such as our sense of hearing, sight or touch. For example, if someone describes a vehicle as a 'car', we would accept this description if the vehicle complies with the criteria we normally associate with a car. A two-wheeled vehicle would not normally meet such criteria, and hence we would not accept its inclusion in the category of a 'car'. What we have done here is to apply the evidence of our senses, in this case the evidence of sight, to establish whether an object falls into a particular category.

Advice for students 16.1

We often think of research as a process which contributes to human knowledge and understanding. When we use language such as this, it can be very tempting to think of research as adding to our ideas of truth. However, when you are writing your dissertation, it is preferable to be cautious when speaking about the concept 'truth'. Rather than writing that 'this theory contributes to our understanding of truth', it would be more philosophically accurate to suggest that 'this theory helps us to work towards a potentially more accurate understanding of truth'. The difference is nuanced, but nevertheless tangible.

This kind of data, gathered through our senses, is known as empirical data. Some philosophers and researchers regard empirical data as the sole source of evidential justification about the world. Such people are usually termed *empiricists*.

In the above case of the car, what has happened logically is that we have in our minds a set of criteria which define when an object of transport can legitimately be described as a car. We then apply those criteria to new objects in order to determine whether they too can be described as cars. For example, we use our sense of hearing to establish that a vehicle has an engine. We use our sense of sight to establish that a vehicle has wheels and tyres; and we use our sense of touch to establish that the engine generates heat when it has been running for some time. All of this empirical data contributes to the assertion that this vehicle can probably be considered to be a car.

As part of this discussion, it is worth reflecting on the origin of the criteria which we employ to determine whether an object is a car. Empiricists would argue that we are normally confronted by a number of examples of objects which people clearly describe as cars. We then perform a kind of analytic process to try to determine the features such objects have in common. As a result of this empirical analysis, we develop, in effect, a set of tests which we can apply to determine the truth or otherwise of an object actually being a car.

In the case of a qualitative research study, suppose we interview a sample of art students, asking them to discuss what they consider to be their most important problem in their development as artists. To varying degrees, they all claim that their biggest problem is their ability to develop a unique style of painting which is immediately identifiable by other artists and the public. You continue by interviewing other students and exploring this theme in various ways. Some students show you examples of their paintings, pointing out ways in which they have tried to develop a unique style. Eventually you are able to articulate a general statement about the training of art students which encompasses the idea of developing a unique style. The basis of this analysis is essentially empirical since it depends on listening to the accounts of art students and also looking at their creative works, while at the same time listening to their explanations of their creative activity. This process is described in philosophical terms as one of inductive reasoning. It considers a range of empirical data and distils the essence of that data into a general theory about the topic in question. Such a theory can never reflect 'truth' in a certain way. The theory is merely accepted as true as long as it appears to explain new data as the latter emerges. If the theory does not appear to explain new data, then it will need to be amended in order to do so. This process of inductive reasoning is at the heart of grounded theorizing.

Avoiding concepts before the research

We tend to think of qualitative research as involving the sorting and analysis of concepts and data, in order to gradually develop a theory. To do this effectively, one has to start with an idea of the principal topic of the research. One cannot really start the data collection process in a total vacuum, collecting whatever data come to mind. The initial research process has to start somewhere. However, it is important to make a distinction between this process, and that of traditional deductive science. The latter case involves the testing of either a hypothesis or a theory in order to assess its validity, or we might say 'truth'. In qualitative or inductive theorizing, however, we have nothing to test at the beginning. All we possess is a research idea, and a gradually expanding portfolio of data and concepts which we intend to employ to develop a theory. If we are to adhere to the key principles of grounded theory, it is important that we do not anticipate the key facets of the research from the beginning. We must stick to the principle of developing our categories and concepts by means of a continual process of creative analysis. The categories which will ultimately emerge from the data are thus forged from the empirical data.

It is important, however, that in grounded theory we do not pre-judge the concepts and categories which we will find in the data. Qualitative data is voluminous in nature, and needs to be sorted into categories which make sense within this large scope of material. It is important to have at least some idea of the research questions which command your attention, since if this is not the case, then it will be very difficult to construct grounded theories. There is, however, a key distinction between trying to test precise concepts within a hypothesis, as in deductive methods, and constructing theories and hypotheses by means of an analytic process.

Grounded theorizing has become very popular as an analytic method, but there remain one or two potential drawbacks with the approach. If you are conducting grounded theory analysis on your own, there is always the danger of bias occurring during the theorizing process. It is usually wise to enlist the help of one or two other analysts who can provide counterbalancing idea, and perhaps improve the objectivity of the analysis. Linked to the question of potential bias is that of generalization. One of the long-standing issues of inductive methodologies are the problems which arise from the use of small samples. The principal difficulty is that it remains problematic to apply conclusions drawn from a small sample to a wider context. However, by applying similar grounded theory analyses in a different but related situation, it is possible to form a judgement as to whether a theory grounded in data from one context can reasonably be applied to another situation.

Theoretical sampling

In quantitative research, the normal procedure with sampling is to reflect carefully upon the planned research design, and then to develop a sampling strategy. This will usually be connected with the overall plan for the methodology, and also with the nature of the research topic. Hence, in a study of teenage gangs, there may well be a sample which is derived from a 'snowball' strategy.

Some members of gangs may not wish to be associated with the activities of gangs and may therefore be reluctant to be a respondent for the research. On the other hand, one gang member, who is happy to participate, may be able to suggest another member who is willing to take part. The entire sampling strategy may thus proceed in this way.

In qualitative research, however, the sampling process tends to be much more randomized and dependent upon the nature of the gradual evolution of the research. For example, in the case mentioned earlier of art students developing a distinctive personal style, sampling may well proceed in the following manner. Several students in the initial sample may well indicate the difficulty they found in developing a personal style. Perhaps one or two students indicated how they selected several well-known artists with a distinctive style, in order to try to develop their own approach to painting. This might lead the researcher to seek out several students who could discuss the influence on them of a particular artist. This further may lead to the identification of other students who had been influenced by the same artist. One student pointed out that informal comments from fellow students were often influential in helping them adapt and individualize their style. In other words, as the researcher gradually developed a theory of individual style in painting, this leads to further ideas for sampling and selecting individual respondents. This approach to sampling is termed *theoretical sampling* and is often associated with grounded theory. As the ideas for the theory gradually evolve, these ideas stimulate further strategies for sampling. This process continues until there is a lack of further ideas for sampling. The provisional theory will then be tested against new data in order to ascertain whether or not it appears to explain that data. If not, then the theory will need to be subject to further revisions. Coyne (1997: 624) and Draucker et al. (2007: 1138) provide further discussion of the nature of theoretical sampling.

Grouping and categorizing of data

Qualitative methods generate a voluminous amount of data. Whether we think of interview research, the use of personal diaries, or biographical research, such methods normally produce a rich and extensive body of data. The main purpose of grounded theory however, is to convert this large body of data into a theory which has a number of important functions.

Philosophically speaking, such a theory is described as 'grounded' because it emerges from this extensive data. It does not, for example, typically reflect the views of the researcher, except perhaps tangentially in the way in which the researcher develops the method for the construction of the theory. A grounded theory has a number of key purposes. It takes the original body of data, and distils from it the essential characteristics which can help people understand the topic. The central features of the data help the researcher to predict how future data could be understood and interpreted. The theory should also be helpful in understanding future data, and linking with theories in related fields in order to build up an understanding of the broad field.

The process of extracting from the data, the key ideas, themes or concepts, is known as coding. Different researchers may well carry out the coding process in their own individual way, and may not necessarily generate precisely the same key ideas. However, the coding process starts by the researcher identifying a concept or idea from the data, and giving this concept a name. Such concepts are often termed categories. Such categories are normally given a relevant name, which helps the researcher to remember the broad nature of the category.

Advice for students 16.2

As you start the process of coding your data and developing categories, it is important to document the analytic process accurately. As you identify new categories, it is important to select relevant names for the new categories, and to be clear yourself why you have allocated certain pieces of data to that category. The reasoning for the latter process should be documented, and subsequently summarized in your dissertation. This ensures that the analytic process for your research is transparent and clear to the reader.

Let us consider, as an example, the study skills required by a new, first-year undergraduate at university. You have collected a lot of interview data and are beginning to identify categories from the data. The first category concerns establishing good working relationships with tutors in order that the undergraduate can have a good understanding of what is expected of them. We might term this first category 'tutor relationship'. This category may include such elements as the student appreciating how to prepare for tutorials; how to structure essays; how to reference academic sources accurately and how to present logical arguments. This strategy of identifying initial categories is often known as open coding.

At this stage, the researcher has no particular preconceptions about the likely nature of the developing categories but allows themself to be influenced only by the evolving analysis of the data. As the researcher continues reading the data, it will be possible to identify further categories. One such category might relate to the ability to plan and design a small-scale research study. This category might be termed 'research planning'. Gradually the number of categories will increase in range and depth, and as the reading of the data continues, it should be possible to include new data and examples in the categories which have been identified. Sometimes there will not be a relevant category within which to include some new data, and in this case a new category will have to be created. The open coding process continues by continually comparing the new data which is read with the categories which have previously been delineated. This procedure is termed the constant comparative method. During this process, the researcher makes notes or memos which suggest ways in which the categories are beginning to reflect the complexity of the process by which undergraduates and tutors are beginning to interact and are slowly developing a relationship structured around the intellectual growth and understanding of the undergraduate. Eventually there will reach a point where as much data as possible has been fitted into existing categories, and equally it does not seem feasible to create any new categories. At this stage there may well be some redundant data which it is not possible to relate to the existing research problem, and at this point this stage of coding analysis can be thought of as completed.

Case study 16.1

Although it is convenient to try to subdivide the process of data analysis and of category creation into discrete stages, it is important not to be too rigid about this. As soon as you think that you might have completed the process of category formation, you realize that further development or analysis might be needed. In fact, with any qualitative analysis study, it is important to retain a certain degree of flexibility.

You may begin to consider that one important feature of academic writing is the ability to identify previous academic work which has been completed in a particular area, and then to build your own writing upon that previous work. You might decide to term this idea, 'academic cohesion' and to regard it as a subset of the category 'tutor relationship'.

In other words, in reality, the process of categorization may continue for the duration of the theory formation, and may involve dividing categories or merging smaller categories. However, in order to begin to create a theory there has to be an increased emphasis upon trying to understand the ways in which the categories affect each other. This process of trying to appreciate the relationships between categories is sometimes termed axial coding. For example, you may begin to feel that some categories are foundational or fundamental to the developing theory, because from them stem the remainder of the categories. You may feel that, for example, 'tutor relationship' is one such category. As you begin to consider the total theory and its development, you may begin to form the idea of a hierarchy of categories, with several fundamental categories influencing smaller, more specific coded groups.

Although the notion of causality is normally associated with quantitative research, it may also be useful in a qualitative study to try to determine if one category has an influence on the development of other categories. For example, a category concerned with reading academic journal articles and understanding their structure, may have an effect upon the ability of the undergraduate to plan and conduct research studies. When the relationships between categories have been provisionally established, then the next stage of this coding process is to prepare flow charts or algorithms which show, in a graphical manner, the relationships between categories. The flow chart also shows in graphical order the sequence in which categories have an influence upon each other.

In the final stage of the coding process, the researcher produces a clear account of the mechanism of the flow chart diagram, and the number of undergraduates who appear to use it. The account should explain the sequence in which the categories affect each other, and the manner in which they reflect the structure of the overall explanation. The provisional theory which has been developed consists of both the flow chart and also of the written explanation, which elucidates the functioning of the theory.

The final stage of coding is to submit the provisional theory to a testing phase to see if its explanatory mechanisms function well with a new sample of respondents. The researcher selects a new body of respondents who are asked similar questions to the first sample. The data is analysed using the same categories as in the existing flow chart. If the flow chart appears to explain the data from the second sample, then the theory is accepted as provisionally valid. If the theory does not appear to have an explanatory function with the new data, then it is rejected for the time being, until it can be revised in the light of the second sample of data.

When you are analysing qualitative data, the sheer volume of data involved can be a significant problem. It is sometimes difficult to decide which pieces of data are the most significant. Equally, you may find that you have to attach many pieces of data to the same category, making it very difficult to identify individual fragments of data. For these kinds of reason there has been a lot of development in recent years of software packages aimed at analysing qualitative data. These packages are generally known under the collective name of: 'computer-assisted qualitative data analysis software (CAQDAS)'. As with all research-focused data analysis software, they provide great assistance with the mechanical aspects of the research process, but it is important to remember that in the final analysis it is the researcher who provides the instructions in relation to the software. Ultimately it is the researcher who reads the data, and allocates segments of it to different categories. The researcher can identify categories in advance of the coding process, or alternatively can develop categories while the coding is proceeding. Strictly speaking, however, the latter strategy is more in harmony with the philosophy of qualitative methods. There are many different types of software available for qualitative analysis, but in general they employ the same types of function. In exploring a large amount of data, they will generally save you a considerable amount of time with activities such as coding. The consistency obtained when using computers is also a help with increasing the validity of the analysis. The flexibility of the use of computers encourages a deep analysis of data, and an emphasis upon its richness. Computer packages can be very useful in enabling the researcher to quickly and efficiently access data segments filed under categories. They also enable the presentation of categories in innovative forms, such as coding algorithms.

Nevertheless, there are some disadvantages in the use of software. First, software packages may need an investment of time in order for the researcher to become familiar with their use. The packages are also developing their own terminology, with, for example, the term 'node' being employed as a synonym for coding category. Overall, CAQDAS packages have improved the capacity of the researcher to analyse non-numerical data, and to investigate connections between categories and nodes. However, it is important to remember that at the end of the day, the data analysis is still conducted by the researcher, and not by the computer software.

Ecological validity

One of the potential problems with grounded theory studies, and with the theories which emerge from such studies, is that they may not relate very closely to everyday life or to real, practical situations. Where this occurs, the lack of applicability to the real world is referred to as an absence of *ecological validity*. Let us consider why this situation may develop.

In some social science research, it may not always be possible to gather data from actual, real-life situations. This may be particularly true of situations involving the professional training of people for different occupations. For example, teacher-training students practise teaching in a classroom where the usual teacher sits to offer help and advice. Trainee social workers may participate in artificially constructed case conference situations in order to examine issues involved when the problems of clients are being discussed; and medical professionals may practise their skills under the close supervision of experienced colleagues. However, these situations, while possessing some of the features of the real world, do not completely reflect reality. Research data provided by such simulated situations may not reflect, for example, the pressures and tensions of the real world. When data is collected in such contexts, there is the danger that it may have limited ecological validity; or in other words may not reflect real-life situations as closely as it might. It is important to be aware of this possibility and if necessary to evaluate it in any discussion of the validity of the research. Further discussion on ecological validity is available in Schmuckler (2001: 420).

Conclusion

I hope this book has been of use to you in planning your research study, whether you are coming towards the end of your first degree or are working on your postgraduate dissertation. One of the main qualities which examiners look for in a dissertation is that it should be written and structured in a logical, planned way. Arguably the best way to do this is to start with a clearly expressed research question, and then to articulate the most appropriate way of investigating that topic. You should do your best to explain the reasons for selecting your particular methodology, and set these down in a logical, precise order. If you follow this strategy from the beginning, it is likely to create a good impression in the mind of the examiner. However, it is also very important that your choice of methodology is one with which you have a degree of competence. There is little or nothing to be gained by selecting a methodology which you do not fully understand.

Qualitative methods have become very popular in recent years, partly because they probably appear to require relatively little technical skill in comparison perhaps with the statistical complexities of quantitative analysis. However, in some ways, this difference in complexity can be deceptive.

Case study 16.2

Qualitative methods such as interviews are very complex in their own way, for example, in terms of the nomenclature used. When writing about a qualitative study, it is important to employ the correct terminology, to evaluate the difficulties of using small samples, and to make it clear why you have selected certain sections of data, and not others.

Qualitative data and research do, however, have many advantages for the student researcher. If you have to write a long dissertation or research study, then one of the eternal problems is to make sure that you have sufficient data. You may be committed to writing a certain number of words, and if this is the case, then you will probably not have a problem if you are using qualitative data. In the case of quantitative data, however, there may be a problem. As you analyse questionnaires, the data often condenses into a few key numerical results, which although they may be interesting, may not generate sufficient volume of discussion for your dissertation.

Qualitative data provides you with a wealth of quotations which can be useful for analysis, and even a small number of respondents can often generate enough data for a long dissertation. Neither does the data collection phase of the research take a long time.

Finally, may I wish you well with your research. I am sure you will find your qualitative study interesting to carry out, and that the data you collect will provide you with useful insights into your research topic.

Learning content

In this chapter you should have become familiar with the following ideas:

- computer-assisted qualitative data analysis software (CAQDAS)
- ecological validity
- empiricists
- grounded theory
- social constructivism
- theoretical sampling

References

Alshenqeeti, H. (2014) 'Interviewing as a data collection method: A critical review', *English Linguistics Research*, 3(1): 39–45.

Anderson, L. (2006) 'Analytic autoethnography', *Journal of Contemporary Ethnography*, 35(4): 373–95.

Aranda, K. (2018) *Feminist Theories and Concepts in Healthcare: An Introduction to Qualitative Research*. London: Red Globe.

Bhopal, R. (2004) 'Glossary of terms relating to ethnicity and race: For reflection and debate', *Journal of Epidemiology and Community Health*, 58(6): 441–5.

Bowman, D., Spicer, J. and Iqbal, R. (2012) *Informed Consent: A Primer for Clinical Practice*. Cambridge: Cambridge University Press.

Bransford, C.L. (2006) 'The use of critical ethnography in managed mental health care settings', *The Journal of Sociology and Social Welfare*, 33(4): 173–92.

Chan, Z.C.Y., Fung, Y-L. and Chien, W-T. (2013) 'Bracketing in phenomenology: Only undertaken in the data collection and analysis process?', *The Qualitative Report*, 18(30): 1–9.

Clarke, C. (2009) 'Paths between positivism and interpretivism: An appraisal of Hay's *Via Media*', *Politics*, 29(1): 28–36.

Cochran-Smith, M. and Fries, M.K. (2001) 'Sticks, stones and ideology: The discourse of reform in teacher education', *Educational Researcher*, 30(8): 3–15.

Coyne, I.T. (1997) 'Sampling in qualitative research: purposeful and theoretical sampling: Merging or clear boundaries?', *Journal of Advanced Nursing*, 26: 623–30.

Darlaston-Jones, D. (2007) 'Making connections: The relationship between epistemology and research methods', *The Australian Community Psychologist*, 19(1): 19–27.

Dickson-Swift, V., James, E., Kippen, S. and Liamputtong, P. (2007) 'Doing sensitive research: What challenges do qualitative researchers face?', *Qualitative Research*, 7(3): 327–53.

Draucker, C.B. et al. (2007) 'Pearls, pith and provocation: Theoretical sampling and category development in grounded theory', *Qualitative Health Research*, 17(8): 1137–48.

Dyer, H. (2016) *The Little Book of Feminism*. Chichester: Summersdale.

Edlund, M.. Lindwall, L., von Post, I. and Lindström, U.A. (2013) 'Concept determination of human dignity', *Nursing Ethics*, 20(8): 851–60.

Edmondson, A.C. and McManus, S.E. (2007) 'Methodological fit in management field research', *Academy of Management Review*, 32(4): 1155–79.

Etikan, I., Musa, S.A. and Alkassim, R.S. (2016) 'Comparison of convenience sampling and purposive sampling', *American Journal of Theoretical and Applied Statistics*, 5(1): 1–4.

Firat, A.F. and Venkatesh, A. (1995) 'Liberatory postmodernism and the reenchantment of consumption', *The Journal of Consumer Research*, 22(3): 239–67.

Freire, P. (2007) *Pedagogy of the Oppressed*. New York: Continuum.

Friedan, B. (2010) *The Feminine Mystique*. London: Penguin.

Gergen, K.J. (2015) *An Invitation to Social Construction* (3rd edn). London: Sage.

Glaser, B.G. and Strauss, A.L. (1967) *The Discovery of Grounded Theory: Strategies for Qualitative Research*. Chicago: Aldine.

Gottfried, H. (ed.) (1996) *Feminism and Social Change: Bridging Theory and Practice*. Urbana, IL: University of Illinois Press.

Hammond, R.A. and Axelrod, R. (2006) 'The evolution of ethnocentrism', *Journal of Conflict Resolution*, 50(6): 926–36.

Hancock, D.R. and Algozzine, B. (2017) *Doing Case Study Research: A Practical Guide for Beginning Researchers* (3rd edn). New York: Teachers College Press.

Hart, J. (2006)'Women and feminism in higher education scholarship: An analysis of three core journals', *The Journal of Higher Education*, 77(1): 40–61.

Hibbin, R.A., Samuel, G. and Derrick, G.E. (2018) 'From "a fair game" to "a form of covert research": Research ethics committee members' differing notions of consent and potential risk to participants within social media research', *Journal of Empirical Research on Human Research Ethics*, 13(2): 149–59.

Honer, A. and Hitzler, R. (2015) 'Life-world-analytical ethnography: A phenomenology-based research approach', *Journal of Contemporary Ethnography*, 44(5): 544–62.

Hossain, F.M.A. (2014) 'A critical analysis of empiricism', *Open Journal of Philosophy*, 4(3): 225–30.

Hyers, L.L. (2018) *Diary Methods: Understanding Qualitative Research*. New York: Oxford University Press.

Katz, J. (2002) 'Social ontology and research strategy', *Theoretical Criminology*, 6(3): 255–78.

Keen, S. (2016) 'Life writing and the empathetic circle', *Concentric: Literary and Cultural Studies*, 42(2): 9–26.

Kinzel, K. and Kusch, M. (2018) 'De-idealizing disagreement, rethinking relativism', *International Journal of Philosophical Studies*, 26(1): 40–71.

Kolb, D.A. (1983) *Experiential Learning: Experience as the Source of Learning and Development*. Englewood Cliffs, NJ: Prentice Hall.

Koopman, O. (2015) 'Phenomenology as a potential methodology for subjective knowing in science education research', *The Indo-Pacific Journal of Phenomenology*, 15(1): 1–10.

Kotarba, J.A. (2014) 'Symbolic interaction and applied social research: A focus on translational science research', *Symbolic Interaction*, 37(3): 412–25.

Kuzmanić, M. (2009) 'Validity in qualitative research: Interview and the appearance of truth through dialogue', *Horizons of Psychology*, 18(2): 39–50.

Ladner, S. (2016) *Practical Ethnography: A Guide to Doing Ethnography in the Private Sector*. Abingdon: Routledge.

Letherby, G. (2003) *Feminist Research in Theory and Practice*. Buckingham: Open University Press.

Lewis, D. (2008) 'Using life histories in social policy research: The case of third sector/public sector boundary crossing', *Journal of Social Policy*, 37(4): 559–78.

Lietz, C.A. and Zayas, L.E. (2010) 'Evaluating qualitative research for social work practitioners', *Advances in Social Work*, 11(2): 188–202.

Long, T. and Johnson, M. (2007) *Research Ethics in the Real World: Issues and Solutions for Health and Social Care*. Edinburgh: Churchill Livingstone.

Lopes, C.S., Rodrigues, L.C. and Sichieri, R. (1996) 'The lack of selection bias in a snowball sampled case-control study on drug abuse', *International Journal of Epidemiology*, 25(6): 1267–70.

MacDonald, C. (2012) 'Understanding participatory action research: A qualitative research methodology option', *Canadian Journal of Action Research*, 13(2): 34–50.

Marshall, M.N. (1996) 'The key informant technique', *Family Practice*, 13(1): 92–7.

McLellan, E., MacQueen, K.M. and Neidig, J.L. (2003) 'Beyond the qualitative interview: Data preparation and transcription', *Field Methods*, 15(1): 63–84.

Meyers, R.G. (2014) *Understanding Empiricism*. Abingdon: Routledge.

Moerer-Urdahl, T. and Creswell, J.W. (2004) 'Using transcendental phenomenology to explore the "ripple effect" in a leadership mentoring program', *International Journal of Qualitative Methods*, 3(2): 19–35.

Morse, J.M. and Chung, S.E. (2003) 'Toward holism: The significance of methodological pluralism', *International Journal of Qualitative Methods*, 2(3): 13–20.

Nyumba, T.O., Wilson, K., Derrick, C.J. and Mukherjee, N. (2018) 'The use of focus group discussion methodology: Insights from two decades of application in conservation', *Methods in Ecology and Evolution*, 9: 20–32.

Oliver, P. (2015) *Sociology: A Complete Introduction*. London: Hodder and Stoughton.

Palaganas, E.C., Sanchez, M.C., Molintas, M.P. and Caricativo, R.D. (2017) 'Reflexivity in qualitative research: A journey of learning', *The Qualitative Report*, 22(2): 426–38.

Poland, B.D. (1995) 'Transcription quality as an aspect of rigor in qualitative research', *Qualitative Enquiry*, 1(3): 290–310.

Rhoads, R.A., Berdan, J. and Toven-Lindsey, B. (2013) 'The Open Courseware movement in higher education: Unmasking power and raising questions about the movement's democratic potential.' *Educational Theory*, 63(1): 87–109.

Sartre, J-P. (2007) *Existentialism Is a Humanism*. New Haven, CT: Yale University Press.

Schmuckler, M.A. (2001) 'What is ecological validity? A dimensional analysis', *Infancy*, 2(4): 419–36.

Schwartz-Shea, P. and Yanow, D. (2012) *Interpretive Research Design: Concepts and Processes*. Abingdon: Routledge.

Seidman, I. (2019) *Interviewing as Qualitative Research: A Guide for Researchers in Education and the Social Sciences*. New York: Teachers College Press.

Sokolowski, R. (2000) *Introduction to Phenomenology*. Cambridge: Cambridge University Press.

Stake, R.E. (1995) *The Art of Case Study Research*. London: Sage.

Steinbeck, J. (1980) *Travels with Charley: In Search of America*. New York: Penguin Random House.

Stryker, S. (2008) 'From Mead to a structural symbolic interactionism and beyond', *Annual Review of Sociology*, 34: 15–31.

Tadajewski, M. (2006) 'Remembering motivation research: Toward an alternative genealogy of interpretive consumer research', *Marketing Theory*, 6(4): 429–66.

Tee, S.R. and Lathlean, J.A. (2004) 'The ethics of conducting a co-operative inquiry with vulnerable people', *Journal of Advanced Nursing*, 47(5): 536–43.

Thomas, G. (2016) *How to Do Your Case Study* (2nd edn). London: Sage.

Thomas, W.I., Znaniecki, F. and Zaretsky, E. (eds) (1996) *The Polish Peasant in Europe and America: A Classic Work in Immigration History*. Urbana, IL: University of Illinois Press.

Välimäki, T., Vehviläinen-Julkunen, K. and Pietilä, A-M. (2007) 'Diaries as research data in a study on family caregivers of people with Alzheimer's disease: Methodological issues', *Journal of Advanced Nursing*, 59(1): 68–76.

Veil, S. (2009) *A Life*, trans. T. Black. London: Haus.

Ward, G. (2010) *Understand Postmodernism*. London: Hodder Education.

Webster, J.W. (2016) '"Filling the gaps": Oral histories and underdocumented populations in *The American Archivist*, 1938–2011', *The American Archivist*, 79(2): 254–82.

Wiles, R., Crow, G., Heath, S. and Charles, V. (2008) 'The management of confidentiality and anonymity in social research', *International Journal of Social Research Methodology*, 11(5): 417–28.

Yow, V.R. (2015) *Recording Oral History: A Guide for the Humanities and Social Sciences* (3rd edn). London: Rowman & Littlefield.

Index

Page numbers with 't' are tables.